Living Together

Sanghadevi

Living Together

WINDHORSE PUBLICATIONS

Published by Windhorse Publications
11 Park Road, Birmingham, B13 8AB

© Sanghadevi 2003

Printed by Interprint Ltd, Marsa, Malta
Cover design: Sagarapriya
Cover images: 'Tokyo, Japan' by Piecework Productions / Getty Images;
'Square Patterns in Red' © PhotoDisc

British Library Cataloguing in Publication Data:
A catalogue record for this book is available from the British Library.
ISBN 1 899579 50 8

The right of Sanghadevi to be identified as the author of this work
has been asserted by her in accordance with the Copyright, Designs
and Patents Act 1988

Since this work is intended for a general readership, most Pali and
Sanskrit words have been transliterated without the diacritical marks
that would have been appropriate in a work of a more scholarly nature.

The publishers acknowledge with gratitude permission to quote from
the following:
pp. 43, 52–3 from I.B. Horner (trans), *The Collection of the Middle Length
Sayings*, Pali Text Society, London 1976. Reproduced with the permission
of the publisher.
pp. 44, 89, 91–2 © Bhikkhu Bodhi 1995, 2001. Reprinted from *The Middle
Length Discourses of the Buddha: A Translation of the Majjhima Nikāya*, with
permission of Wisdom Publications, 199 Elm St., Somerville, MA 02144,
U.S.A. www.wisdompubs.org

CONTENTS

About the Author

Sanghadevi was born Christine Seymour in London in 1954. She first made contact with Buddhism while she was a student at the University of Leicester, where she gained an honours degree in Biological Sciences in 1975 and then returned to London to become more involved with the Friends of the Western Buddhist Order.

Sanghadevi joined her first community in 1976, and a year later she was ordained and given her Buddhist name, which means 'one who illuminates the spiritual community'. She has continued to live communally with other women ever since – in London, South and North Wales, and now in Birmingham. She has been involved in various projects that develop living and working situations for Buddhist women, including the foundation of Taraloka Women's Retreat Centre in Wales. In 1989, Sangharakshita, the head of the Western Buddhist Order, asked her and two other women to conduct ordinations for women, and in August 2000 he handed on responsibility for ordination to a College of Public Preceptors, of which Sanghadevi is a member.

Although based in Britain, Sanghadevi spends much of her time in North America and Australasia conducting retreats for women who wish to join the Order. In her spare time she enjoys photography, sketching, and painting.

PREFACE

Living Together – the third publication in this series 'Living a Buddhist Life' – looks at what is perhaps the most fundamental aspect of our lives. Where and how we live is the backdrop to all our activities and influences us daily in overt and subtle ways. Home and home life is associated with security, intimacy, relaxation, company; home is where we sleep, eat, make love, raise families; it is where we look for many of our human needs to be met; it is where we share our lives with others. The author, Sanghadevi, looks at this basic human activity of living together from a Buddhist perspective, in the context of community living, as an opportunity for spiritual growth.

All the necessary elements are there – oneself, other people, time together on a daily basis, and – potentially – insight into the lives of others: their difficulties and woes as well as their joys. In whatever way we choose to live, whether with others or on our own, we can create a more satisfying life for ourselves and more harmonious relationships with others.

I have lived communally or collectively since leaving my family home; mostly with other women. In some ways I see the direction of my life as a search for true community, not thought out to begin with, but as intuitive impulses. In my early teens it was a community of friends and their friends; a mutual bonding against what seemed to be the narrow world of our parents' lives. In my late teens it was a wider identification with the alternative lifestyles and ideas of my generation; the hippie community with its ethos of freedom from the mortgage, the nuclear family, and the five-day week.

In my early twenties I made the leap of committing myself to the practice of community life and went with a group of friends to set up a commune in the south of Ireland, going 'back to the land', living off what we could grow, sharing all our possessions – money, clothes, books, rooms. It was a brave but misguided attempt. Our anarchic ideals were strongly felt but confused and we did not have the maturity to acknowledge our confusion, or the gap between what we were capable of and those ideals. There were euphoric times, such as when we gathered our first harvest, and times of intense conflict and power struggles. The accumulated tensions resulted in an explosion – and that was the end of the project as a community.

In retrospect, I thought the commune had failed as a community for a number of reasons: there was no coherent common ideal or body of principles that could act as a unifying force; there were tensions both across and between the sexes. There was a 'tyranny of structurelessness' as a later pamphlet described it. These and other reflections led me into my next attempt at a community – living with other women involved in the women's liberation movement. During this period I lived with women who identified as feminists, within a larger feminist community in East London. We were united in our vision of a new world based on feminist values, but after a number of years I became disenchanted again, realizing that much of that sense of unity came from being united against a common enemy, that of 'patriarchy'. In the late seventies and early eighties many attempts at alternative lifestyles, and the movements associated with them, disintegrated.

It was with some surprise and delight that I discovered the ideal and practice of community living was alive and flourishing when I first made contact with the Friends of the Western Buddhist Order in East London, and to discover that this ideal, though 'new' in the sense that most of the communities had not existed for very long, was based on principles and practices centuries old in the Buddhist tradition. Those principles and practices had been developed to the end of overcoming greed, hatred, and ignorance, not only in the world but, more essentially, in our hearts.

I have since lived for some twenty years with other practising Buddhists. Much of this time has been an attempt to bring 'spiritual community' into being. I cannot say I have lived in peace and harmony for the last twenty years. I can remember one vivid moment when I stood facing a fellow community member, arms akimbo, 'agreeing' that things had got to such an impasse that one of us would have to go. In fact, neither of us left and she became one of my dearest and closest friends with whom I feel I can be completely myself and could share anything and everything.

I am still exploring how the process of living in community, of sharing my life with others who see this way of life as a context for human and spiritual growth, can loosen the chains of greed, hatred, and ignorance. My life has become richer as a result, but there is always further to go. In this book, in essence, what Sanghadevi gives us are the ingredients for a successful community: a shared vision, consistent kindness, ethical awareness, trust, cooperation, and a commitment to communication. These ingredients are simple to list but difficult to live out. Sanghadevi breathes life into them, informed by her breadth of experience of community living over the years.

By focusing on our actions of body, speech, and mind in our home lives we are not confining the benefits to those we live with; rather we will be better able to bring those qualities of friendliness, awareness, and a willingness to tolerate and share into the wider arena of our lives and society.

Maitreyi
Tiratanaloka
Wales
September 2002

INTRODUCTION

A community is about people living together, basing their shared lives on common values and, in the case of Buddhist communities, a commitment to Buddhist practice. I would like to share with you my experience of endeavouring to live a spiritual life in the context of community for the last twenty-five years. By sharing some of my experiences of community living, I hope to stimulate awareness of the creative possibilities of living with others, particularly of living in community with those who share the same spiritual values. I also hope that those who already live in this way, whether newly so or with many years' experience, will also find something of interest in what I have to say, and I hope they will be encouraged to engage ever more fully in the challenges and joys of living in community.

During those last twenty-five years I have lived with many different people in a range of communities. Some have lasted a few weeks (in the context of a Buddhist retreat), some many years. It's this variety of experience that I've drawn on to write this book.

Let's start with a shorter period of time. While I was working on this book, I was on retreat for a period of five weeks with twenty-six other women in what had once been a monastery, nestling in the Tuscan hills of Italy. We were all practising Buddhists. Indeed, many of the women present on the retreat were about to undergo ordination into the Western Buddhist Order.[1] We effectively lived as a community for those five weeks, sharing a common way of life. We meditated together, ate together, studied and listened to Dharma talks together, performed various Buddhist rituals together, as well as various practical chores, and so on. It was a rich and rewarding time; the muses descended and people composed and shared poetry and song. An eleven-foot-high stupa manifested one day in the anteroom to the shrine room. The shrine, dedicated to the Buddha, became ever more beautiful and imaginative. The silence we observed for periods of the retreat deepened and grew in significance. Friendliness and kindness flowed between us. For some of those present, it was their first extended experience of living with fellow spiritual practitioners. The benefits of increased friendliness, cooperation, creativity, and energy were manifest for all and our shared spiritual purpose was brought increasingly into focus. I imagine we each returned, as I did, to our various living situations around the world with a much clearer sense of what we were trying to do, spiritually speaking, and with our energies more galvanized to get on with the task.

On a longer-term basis, one of my most rewarding community experiences to date has been living and working at Taraloka: a women's community cum retreat centre in northern Wales, founded in November 1985 by myself and three other women.

I found it rewarding for several reasons. In great part, there was a relatively high degree of continuity in terms of who lived there over the seven years I was there. This meant we were able to build up a certain depth of communication based on increasing mutual knowledge and understanding. Much of my community experience until that time had involved a shifting pool of people who moved on after about a year. The other main factor was that we had a shared project: that of running a retreat centre. This gave us a very clear overall purpose to engage our energies. It meant that we shared our lives since we all lived and worked in the same place. Moreover, the retreats we led, organized, or supported regularly fed back ideas and inspiration into our community life.

It was during my time at Taraloka that I was introduced to one particular story from the time of the Buddha's life, and realized how far-reaching living with others could be. It seems fitting then to use this story of the Anuruddhas as a framework for an exploration of community living and of why it can be a support to spiritual practice.

An Early Buddhist Community

In an early Buddhist text, we come across the story of three young men, Nandiya, Kimbila, and Anuruddha (otherwise referred to as the Anuruddhas), living together in a jungle clearing. Some time previously, they had decided to leave their family homes and adopt the life of wandering mendicants in order to devote themselves to spiritual practice under the guidance of the Buddha. At the time of this story, they are living together in the forest. They are clothed in simple robes, sewn together from cast-off rags and dyed ochre with earth. Apart from these, they have virtually no material possessions: just an alms bowl and a few other basic items. They spend their days in meditation and reflection in the shade of trees, sharing basic chores such as collecting water and gathering almsfood from villages in the vicinity. Every few days they meet together in the cool of the evening to review their spiritual practice in the light of the Buddha's teachings. The rest of the time they observe silence.

One day the Buddha comes to visit. Anuruddha is the first to become aware of his arrival. He sets off to find his two friends in order to tell them the good news and encourage them to come with him to meet the Buddha. They are delighted their teacher is paying them a visit. As he makes his way through the trees to their clearing, they go forward to greet him. Soon the Buddha is seated in their midst, and after making some general enquiries about their welfare, he asks them whether they are living together in a friendly, harmonious manner, 'as milk and water blend, regarding one another with the eye of affection'.[2] They assure him they are and that the friendliness they feel towards one another has grown out of reflection on their good fortune to be living with such fellow Dharma-farers. As the conversation develops, it becomes clear that the way they live together is very much part of their spiritual practice; indeed, it is an important support to it.

A pleasant, even inspiring, story – but what relevance does it have today? The simple forest-dwelling life of these young men is surely a far cry from the conditions of modern society. Even if it were still possible to live in such a way, how many of us would really want to? After all, the Anuruddhas took what many of us would consider a rather drastic step. They left behind friends and family. They gave up all their worldly possessions. They turned their backs on the concerns of the world: working for a living, marriage, raising a family, political intrigues, and so on.

Yet despite the very different conditions under which the Anuruddhas lived, we can learn from them some useful tips about what is involved in community living, for that is what the Anuruddhas were: a community. As I have already said, communities are about people: a number of people living together and sharing their life together on the basis of common values. The Anuruddhas had chosen to live together because they shared the same spiritual ideal, the glorious vision of human Enlightenment, of which the Buddha was a shining example. Moreover, they were dedicated to putting the Buddha's teachings into practice in their own lives in order to gain Enlightenment themselves. As a means to help reach this goal, they saw it as a great benefit to live with fellow spiritual practitioners.

What a Spiritual Community can Offer Today

It is not easy to make spiritual headway under the conditions of modern society, where material values tend to be held more highly than spiritual values and where cynicism tends to undermine faith. Moreover, there is much to distract us from our overall purpose; there is so much on offer materially, culturally, even spiritually. Even in the time of the Buddha, when life was far simpler than it is now, and when Indian society was sympathetic and supportive towards those following a full-time spiritual life, considerable spiritual effort was required to ensure progress. It is useful to remember that there were still all manner of inner obstacles to contend with, even if the outer ones were less obstructive. For example, we read of the Anuruddhas suffering from doubt, sloth, consternation, elation, distress, too much energy, not enough energy, craving, and so on. Quite a collection! No wonder they found it helpful to live together, mutually encouraging one another to keep going despite the obstacles they had to face in their efforts to transform their consciousness. Given that the conditions of Western society are not as supportive to a spiritual life as they have been in times past, nor are they as supportive as they were in north-eastern India 2,500 years ago at the time of the Buddha, perhaps we can begin to imagine why it might be helpful today to live with other spiritual practitioners.

This is something my teacher, Sangharakshita, realized quite early on in his work to create a new, spiritually vital Buddhist movement in the West. He noticed how people blossomed when they came together with others to meditate and study the Dharma, whether for a few days or a week or more. He also noticed how quickly that positivity and clarity of purpose dissipated when people returned to their everyday lives.[3]

If you have been on some retreats yourself, you may have noticed the emergence of very good intentions, only to have them dwindle with time. Take, for example, setting up a daily meditation practice. On retreat, there may be several sessions of meditation each day, and this contributes to a build-up of positivity and clarity. We also need to keep up our meditation when we are not on retreat. Some people set up such a routine quite easily, whether they live with others who meditate or not, but for many of us this isn't the case. We may come back from a retreat thinking, 'Yes, this is what is important in my life. This is what I should do. I will rearrange my life so that I can meditate each morning for twenty minutes before I go to work.' We get off to a good start but then one morning, after a particularly late night and a rather trying day at the office, we don't get up when the alarm goes. 'Never mind, I'll fit it in later in the day,' we think. But something happens, we bump into an old friend on the way home from work and decide to go for a drink. One thing leads to another and before you know it you've had another late night and feel disinclined yet again to respond to the alarm next morning calling you to meditate. Over the ensuing weeks, meditation gradually becomes more sporadic until, in the end, it drops away altogether (unless perhaps you're attending local meditation classes).

There could be other reasons why our good intentions fall by the wayside. Perhaps we lack the courage to be a bit different from our current social circle. I remember for myself that this concern evaporated when I moved into my first community back in 1976. The three other women all meditated and, for the first time, I readily established a daily meditation practice of my own. Until then I had only meditated sporadically since being taught meditation two years earlier. I never felt very comfortable meditating in a shared house where the others didn't meditate. I sensed that my housemates found my interest in vegetarianism and meditation a little weird. I would sometimes sit quietly on the floor in my room with the lights turned low and a candle and incense burning – but I didn't want to put a note on my door asking them not to disturb me. Hence, I didn't do any formal meditation. Once I was living with others who also meditated regularly, it felt easy to tell them that was what I was doing.

My experience matched that of others: that more supportive conditions for ongoing spiritual practice were needed within the wider society. Such conditions would both help people to stay more readily in contact with the spiritual aspirations they espoused and also support and encourage putting them into practice. In this way, over time, it would be possible for a deep and lasting spiritual transformation of the individual to take place.

I would like to share the benefits I have enjoyed from living with others, as well as look at the challenges. The following chapters therefore go into the importance and value of loving-kindness and how it contributes to the strength of any community. I also discuss some of the personal challenges that arise from living in a community: the daily practice of ethics, working with pride, cooperation, learning to create harmony without losing one's own voice, and the many positive outcomes of community living such as simplicity, sharing, caring for the environment, developing mutual responsibility, and the joy of good communication.

1

GETTING STARTED

A Shared Ideal

What draws people to live communally may be quite
varied. It could be financial expediency: it is often
cheaper than living on one's own. Alternatively, it could
be that one or more people at the core of a community
have some kind of vision for the community that draws
people in. For example, they may envisage a rural community that is self-sufficient through organic farming
and cottage industries. Or there may be a set of spiritual
values at the core of a vision. Most, if not all, of the major
world religions have at one time or another inspired
groups of people to set up a shared life together based
in a common faith. It is such spiritually-based communities that have tended to pass the test of time and
continue down the centuries.

The Anuruddhas chose to live together because they
shared the same spiritual ideal, what Buddhists call the
Three Jewels. They had 'gone for Refuge' to the Three

Jewels. These very same ideals have formed the basis of all the communities I have lived in over the years, for, like the Anuruddhas, I am a practising Buddhist. So let's look briefly at these Three Jewels.

First comes the Buddha jewel, the ideal of human Enlightenment. The Anuruddhas had the good fortune to live in the presence of a human being, Siddhartha Gautama, who had become Enlightened, who had become a Buddha. As a young man, Gautama had gone forth from the household life just as these three had now done. He was grappling with the meaning of life in the face of a vivid awareness of the human predicament wherein everyone must eventually become ill, grow old, and die. He felt compelled to seek a permanent and satisfactory solution to this predicament. Studying and practising intensively under various spiritual teachers he swiftly reached their levels of spiritual attainment but realized that none of these states represented the ultimate truth, for all these 'truths' were dependent upon conditions and therefore impermanent. Consequently, Gautama continued his quest on his own. Eventually, he broke through into an altogether new dimension of being and consciousness characterized by perfect wisdom and boundless compassion. This he knew to be Reality, the Truth. He adopted the title 'Buddha', which means one who is awake. Thus the Buddha came to embody what was possible for any human being should they be sufficiently determined: the understanding of Reality and consequent Enlightenment.

Then there is the Dharma jewel. The word 'Dharma' is rich in meaning. In this context, its first meaning is 'Truth' or 'Reality as it is in itself'. Secondly, it means all those teachings and methods that are in harmony with Reality and, as such, conduce to Enlightenment. One of the Buddha's major contributions was to make clear the principles on which spiritual practice should be founded if others were to gain Enlightenment. He also delineated numerous overlapping methods of practice and demonstrated to what extent popular methods of the time did or did not conduce to Enlightenment. Over the centuries, a vast wealth of teachings or Dharma have grown out of the Buddha's original body of teaching from those who have followed in his footsteps and come to know the Truth for themselves.

Lastly, there is the Sangha jewel. When the Buddha first gained Enlightenment, he was on his own. There were no other human beings who had discovered what he had discovered. However, there were plenty of people seeking the truth, seeking the meaning of life. He soon set about sharing his discovery with some of these people, and it was not long before others gained Enlightenment too. These Enlightened individuals were united in their common allegiance to the Buddha and the Dharma. Through taking him as their refuge and reliance, they had come to experience for themselves what he had experienced, and they formed the early 'sangha' or spiritual community.[4] These other Enlightened individuals were themselves a source of inspiration and more and more people wished to follow in their footsteps; going for Refuge not only to the Buddha and Dharma but now also to the Sangha. Anuruddha, Nandiya, and Kimbila had themselves each taken this step. They had gone for Refuge to the transcendental Sangha – to all those who had gained insight into the true nature of things and whose progress towards Buddhahood was certain. At the same time, they also became part of the wider body of the Sangha, comprising people like themselves who aspired to, but who had not yet entered upon, the transcendental path.[5] The Sangha jewel still shines in the world today.

Taking the Plunge

We may come across other people who hold similar ideals to us, but this does not automatically mean we will be keen to live with them. This may be a matter of temperament – some people are solitary characters – or it could be because of our field of work: perhaps we work night shifts on a regular basis, and it is hard to imagine how this would fit in with a communal lifestyle. Then again, we may have no wish to change our current lifestyle, or feel it is appropriate to, at least not at the moment.

People are different and, as in so many areas of life, what attracts one person does not necessarily attract another. There is little point in moving into a community if your heart is not really behind it. You can't do it, based solely on an ideal, if you have little feeling for living with other people. Sometimes we do things because we think we should, or 'it would be good for us', but if we are not sufficiently behind the decision, it won't work. Living with other people is a practice, it involves work, it is like anything in life that is truly rewarding: it involves effort. So unless we are really behind it, there won't be much energy available to work with the challenges that will inevitably arise alongside the many joys that come from living with others.

When I first made contact with a sangha of people practising the Dharma, I was something of a loner. I tended to move through groups of people, never sticking with any one group for very long. I was looking for spiritual meaning in my life. The various people I met either didn't seem to share my urgency to find a spiritual path – or they were quite happy with their existing theistic faith system, a system I had consciously rejected some years before. I eventually encountered practitioners of the Dharma in the context of the FWBO, one of many different sanghas we can currently find in the world. I felt an immediate resonance, not only with the Dharma and the way it was put across by the founder of this particular Buddhist movement, but also with the people I met. I knew that at last I had found a bunch of people I wanted to get to know. At the same time, I was aware that it wasn't going to be particularly easy for me to start building deeper relationships, for I was in some respects quite a shy, even fearful, sort of person.

Making the decision to move into a community didn't happen straightaway. Indeed, the opportunity arose a couple of times before I finally took the plunge. It probably felt a bit scary to consider making such a move.

Then one Sunday afternoon my doorbell rang. There on the doorstep stood a young man I knew from the local sangha. He had come to tell me that a place was about to become available in a local community. This time I knew more or less instantly that I would do it. It's hard to say exactly why; it simply felt right. I still hardly knew the other people involved but I had by then built up more of a working knowledge of the sangha and the values on which it was based. Also, my living circumstances had recently changed and were not particularly satisfactory, so perhaps that influenced my decision. Be that as it may, the time had clearly come to take the plunge. Without further ado, I set off later the same afternoon to visit the women who lived in this community in order to let them know I would like to join them, and I moved in very soon afterwards. That was in January 1976 and I have lived in communities of one kind or another ever since, bar a three-month period when I lived on my own.

The Anuruddhas each tell the Buddha it is 'a gain for me, indeed it is well gotten by me, that I am dwelling with such fellow Brahma-farers.' This suggests they have a tangible experience of benefiting from living with one another – that they have put themselves in the right place with the right people at the right time. I too felt this when I moved into that first community. On a very simple level, it was a relief to live with other people who didn't think I was odd; instead I had the support and help that one can find in a community of like-minded people.

2

LEARNING TO LOVE MORE

It is very easy to take people and situations for granted. However, if we feel ourselves to be benefiting from a situation, or even simply see the potential of a situation to benefit us, then, if we are reasonably psychologically healthy, we will want to be in friendly relationship with the people involved. This doesn't just apply to living in a community. It applies more broadly to any situation that involves other people. Indeed, it applies to living in society itself. Friendliness is not only an essential ingredient if we are to live successfully with other people, Buddhist or not. It is also essential to the stability and well-being of society. The media shows us only too graphically the effect of the absence of sufficient friendliness or love between people, from domestic violence to large-scale wars.

I have increasingly come to see the importance of kindness and friendliness in living with others. This lesson is also emphasized in the story of the Anuruddhas.

Those three fellows feel fortunate to be sharing the same spiritual values and go on to tell the Buddha that on account of this, 'friendliness as to acts of body … acts of speech … acts of thought, whether openly or in private, has risen up' in them. Another translation of the story speaks of them 'maintaining bodily acts of loving-kindness' and so on.[6] For the Anuruddhas, the friendliness they experience towards one another develops naturally from their appreciation of having the opportunity to live together.

Many people wish, even pray, for world peace, for the ending of strife and violence, but if they are honest, they would probably admit that their patience gets tested many times a week, if not several times a day. After all, other people can be very trying. Not that they usually mean to be so; it's just what happens when different people with different views bump up against one another. The Buddhist tradition has developed a meditation practice specifically geared to help us develop more fully rounded and thoroughgoing friendliness, not only towards our fellow human beings but to all other living beings. We don't have to be a Buddhist to benefit from this practice, nor do we have to be living in a community, though if we are, it will be helpful to do this meditation regularly. It strengthens and enlarges the scope of our friendliness and helps us to eradicate unhelpful attitudes that hinder our love for others. It is called the Metta Bhavana.

Metta is a key positive emotion. It is not easy to do justice to its meaning with any one English word.

Sometimes it is translated as 'love', 'loving-kindness', or 'universal loving-kindness'. It is a strong, empathetic response to all life that affirms rather than negates the 'being' of others. It is disinterested love that loves another for what they are in themselves rather than for any use or pleasure we can get out of them. So much of our friendship with others is based in pleasure and utility, but metta is completely free of such motives and, consequently, free of attachment. *Bhavana* is much easier to translate: it means 'cultivation' or 'bringing into being'. Put together, we have 'the development of universal loving-kindness'.

There are various ways in which this meditation can be taught. I will tell you about the form used in the FWBO, since that is the one I am most familiar with. First of all, we begin with a stage towards

Ourselves

To genuinely love ourselves, warts and all, can be a challenge for some of us. It doesn't mean we simply accept ourselves, uncritically, with no sense of where we need to work on ourselves. It is more that we come to a realistic view of ourselves that embraces our strengths and weaknesses, our good qualities and our bad habits. We develop a friendly, kindly attitude that encourages good qualities to grow and gives us the strength of character to face and overcome our moral weaknesses. Metta is said to have the same kind of effect on our spiritual being as the sun on a plant; it stimulates spiritual growth just as the sun stimulates organic growth.

If a healthy sense of self-love (or self-metta) is not present, our friendliness towards others is built on shaky foundations. For example, we may become too dependent on others liking us as a substitute for self-metta. Such dependence can lead to our compromising what we really think, for fear of losing their love, or to jealousy of their friendliness to someone else. We may end up hating them if they don't give us the attention we think we need in order to continue to feel okay about ourselves. These kinds of patterns can play themselves out between people whether they live together or not. But when we live together, the stakes are upped through our being in more continuous and intimate contact with several other people – and our capacity to love ourselves (as well as others) in a more mettaful way is put to the test. Other people are like mirrors: their very presence will reflect back to us the limits of our positivity and we will feel the need to change ourselves.

In order to develop this friendly, kindly attitude within and towards ourselves, we wish ourselves well, perhaps repeating the traditional phrases, 'May I be well, may I be happy, may I progress.'

From the basis of self-metta established in the first stage of the Metta Bhavana, we now move on to the second stage of the meditation and focus loving-kindness on

A Friend
This is someone towards whom we already have friendly feelings. Picking such a person makes it easier

to start extending out beyond ourselves, as there is already a natural tendency for positive thoughts and emotions to flow in their direction. This may be a long-standing friend, or someone in the community we feel friendly towards but with whom we have not yet shared much of our life. If it's someone in the community and we choose them on a regular basis, we will notice that it helps us to start building more of a personal friendship with them.

So how do we build loving-kindness towards this friend? We form a vivid impression of this person in our mind and dwell upon our sense of them. We sit with a sense of who they are, their being, and we encourage the feelings of friendliness and kindness we have culti-vated towards ourselves to flow out towards them, wishing them well, wishing them happiness. Here, as with ourselves, the happiness we wish for them is based in the growth of their good qualities and their ability to overcome those attitudes and tendencies in themselves that bring them suffering.

In this stage, we are advised not to focus on certain categories of people. Those considerably older or younger than us may lead us to slip into childlike feel-ings or maternal or paternal feelings. Choosing some-one who is deceased may lead to feelings of grief and loss. A sexual partner is likely to feed affectionate feel-ings coloured by sexual desire. The point here is to open the channels for a new type of emotion to arise, unim-peded by these predictable and familiar ways of relating to others. As the feeling tone of this stage and the previous one lay the ground for all the subsequent stages of the practice, it is important in this stage of the meditation to try to hit the right note.

Having built up a momentum, a rhythm of loving-kindness firstly for ourselves and then a good friend, in the third stage we bring to mind

A Neutral Person

This is someone for whom we don't feel anything in particular, one way or the other. We neither strongly like them nor strongly dislike them. For most of us the majority of the human race falls into this category, so we have plenty of choice here. We will need to use our imagination even more in this stage than in the second stage.

More particularly, if we join a community, there may be several people towards whom we feel like this. If we are honest with ourselves, we're not that bothered one way or the other whether or not we live with them. There may be one or two people in the community that we really want to live with, and others we're not that interested in, but a community doesn't really take off if the inhabitants aren't particularly interested in engaging with one another. If too many people feel indifferent to one another, the community is likely to be a bit flat and lifeless, with not much energy flowing between people. We will need to make efforts to overcome this neutral indifference – Metta Bhavana to the rescue!

To help us in this part of the practice, we notice that not everyone in the community has the same lack of interest in this person as ourselves. There are others who do appreciate and enjoy their company – and this can begin to draw out a more friendly interest from us, so that the 'neutral person' gradually becomes more alive for us. We begin to feel for their humanity and for their potential to grow as we also wish to grow.

So with this growing breadth of loving-kindness, we can move to the fourth stage of the meditation, that of

The Enemy

This could be someone we don't like or who we feel doesn't like us, someone towards whom we definitely feel an element of aversion. This could be quite a settled dislike or it could be a more fleeting irritation. There are many occasions, in living with others, when petty irritations arise; for example, different standards of tidiness, or forgetfulness and carelessness, can be triggers. Within a community, the consequences of such feelings towards another person can lead to unfortunate incidents of harsh or unkind speech, lack of generosity, and so on. If left unaddressed, they may lead to quite serious breakdowns of communication between people. At the very least, they will mar everyone's enjoyment of living together.

It's important to be honest with oneself about what one feels here towards a difficult (for us) person, even if it's not very pleasant. Only then is there the possibility of our taking steps to address our responses and change them. I've lived with a number of people I did not feel immediately drawn towards, even some I have in certain respects felt repelled by. It has often been some aspect of their physical appearance or manner I have taken a dislike to. I have discovered again and again that it is possible to get over these feelings of aversion through focusing on the person in a more rounded way rather than just on the aspect I have taken a dislike to.

And don't think your good friends are safe from your irritation. Even those towards whom we generally feel friendly are likely to end up in the fourth stage sometimes. Perhaps the bus breaks down on our way home and we allow ourselves to slip into a bad mood. We arrive back at the community a short while before supper, tired and hungry and looking forward to a nice meal cooked by one of our fellow community members, someone we rather like and whose company we enjoy. We wander into the kitchen to find no one there and no sign of a meal in progress. Irritation starts to arise in our mind. 'Where is she? Why isn't she cooking?' A few minutes later, our friend turns up, greeting us with a warm smile. 'Hi, welcome home! Sorry, I hope you don't mind, supper will be a bit late. I got caught up in answering some emails.' Looking darkly at her, we mutter something about hoping it's not going to be too late because we've got a phone date at seven o'clock and stomp off. The next morning, when we sit to meditate opposite her, we notice we are still irritated and decide we had better put her in the fourth stage of the Metta Bhavana, although she is usually in the second. We call her to mind and gradually begin to broaden our perspective from the incident that triggered our irritation.

Whether dealing with something like this, or with someone towards whom we have a more entrenched dislike, we endeavour to bring the whole person into view. We begin to focus our attention on what we have in common rather than on our differences. We dwell on the fact that they are human like us, with their sorrows and joys, hopes and aspirations. They too have feelings; unkind words and deeds can hurt them. In addition, they are not deliberately trying to make our life difficult; and even if they are, that is no reason to hate them. We can reflect that it is not going to help either of us if we indulge in negativity. Indeed, this is likely to inflame any anger and irritation. We can also reflect that there are other people who like them, who see other sides to them, and who don't seem to find them as irritating as we do. So we gradually come to a broader appreciation of them, and their capacity to grow and develop. We develop a heartfelt wish that they too will be able to overcome their weaknesses and cultivate their strengths and, in this way, come to experience ever greater happiness and joy.

We're now about to enter the fifth and final stage of the practice. We bring together all four people – ourselves, our friend, the neutral person, and the 'enemy' – in our imagination, and …

We Break the Barriers

We develop equal metta towards all four people. We then gradually expand our awareness in an ever-widening circle to embrace more and more human beings, more and more other living beings, with metta, with heartfelt friendliness. We can really let our imagination go in this stage, experimenting with different ways of connecting with the myriad life forms on Earth. We can also include beings on other planets or in other dimensions if that has meaning for us.

It can be an interesting and rewarding experience in a community if on some days we choose fellow community members for each of the second to fourth stages. Over time, we can get a tangible experience of going beyond the biases in our feelings towards the others in our community and begin to feel more genuinely friendly towards everyone. One community that I lived in for seven years held a community Metta Bhavana once a week. We gathered in the community meditation room and began with the first stage of the Metta Bhavana. Sometimes we then went through the next three stages as I have described, choosing a community member for each category. On other occasions, someone recited the name of each community member and we spent a few minutes extending metta to each person as their name was mentioned. We then moved into the fifth stage and directed metta equally to all eleven community members. After that, we began to expand our metta out further as described above.

Friendliness for All

Over time, through this meditation, I have found that my capacity to respond to others in a friendly way has grown – and not just to those I have lived with. As I mentioned before, in some respects I was quite a shy, even fearful, person when I first encountered the Dharma and began to meditate. I am not like that now. I am much more interested in other people and able to engage with them in a friendly way. In fact, much of the work I do these days revolves around befriending people and encouraging their aspirations to grow. I am also easier to live with, having become more relaxed and friendly!

There is no limit to how far we can go with this meditation. There are so many people on this planet, to say nothing of all the non-human beings as well. There is plenty of scope to extend the range of our friendliness. The aim of the meditation is not simply to have a nice experience on our cushion; it is for us to start behaving differently towards the various people we come into actual contact with over the course of each day, week, month, and year of our life. It ceases to be just certain special people we favour with our love. It becomes all the people we meet on the bus, at the checkout at the supermarket, in the cinema, or the people we speak to on the phone.

As we all know, the world is vast and inhabited by countless beings, human and non-human. Yet we are ill-equipped to handle this knowledge well. Indeed, the vast mass of humanity, to say nothing of all the other myriads of life forms, is for most of us a nameless, faceless statistic. We might not like to admit this, we might even feel an irrational guilt about it, but it is a fact that, for most of us, we have genuine deep feelings of friendliness for very few people, and even then it is often tied in with our own needs. In this respect, I think community living can be a good training ground for enlarging our capacity to love. As I have mentioned, I have lived with many different people from a number of countries over the past twenty-five years. While I have certainly felt personal preferences towards individuals, I don't think these have ever been the basis of the decisions I have made about whom I live with. Therefore, community living has really stretched me to my limits – and yet I have never regretted this choice of lifestyle. It has helped to make me what I am today: a friendlier, kinder person.

We can see the community as a microcosm of the world. Through living with others, we can extend our capacity to love. We learn to love people not because of more superficial likes or familial attachments and obligations but because of shared values that encourage us to rise above our likes and dislikes or our dull indifference.

Another benefit of community living is that we are not so likely to fool ourselves into thinking we have come further in the development of metta than we in fact have. It is only too easy to kid ourselves about how much we love other people when we meet them on our own terms in quite a circumscribed manner: having a quick cup of coffee together once a week, or occasionally going to the cinema. Not so when we are living together all the time. We soon find out how deep our feelings of friendliness run then!

3

REFLECTIONS BACK

As we've already intimated, living with others can bring us face-to-face with our strengths as well as our weaknesses. I'd like to look more particularly at a few of these challenges and how community life can help us to develop them in a positive way. These are: ethical thought and action, pride, and living in harmony rather than just for oneself.

The Fragrant Perfume of Ethics

The Anuruddhas were consistently friendly to one another, whether 'openly or in private'. There was a congruence in their relating with one another. How they thought about one another, how they spoke to one another, how they acted in relation to one another: it all reflected metta, friendliness, whether others were around to see how they were behaving or not.

We, of course, can be rather fickle. We may be friendly to someone's face and then speak of them unkindly behind their back. We may fall into gossip, for example, or we may be helpful to someone when others are watching us and then become more difficult with the same person when no one else is present. We may say one thing and think quite another. It takes a great deal of effort to be consistently friendly in the way the Anuruddhas were. Cultivating metta will help. We also need to think in terms of ethical practice. To maintain bodily, verbal, and mental acts of friendliness or loving-kindness, whether 'openly or in private', is in effect about treating our fellow human beings, our fellow community members, ethically. We can say that metta has an ethical dimension or that metta expresses itself through ethical action. Just as others' behaviour has an effect on us, so does our behaviour affect other people.

Buddhist ethics is an ethics of intention. It is the mental state behind any given action of body, speech, or mind that determines whether the action is ethical or unethical. In Buddhism, ethical is rendered as 'skilful', unethical is rendered as 'unskilful'. The term 'skilful' suggests that we need to apply intelligent awareness to a situation in order to respond appropriately. Those actions that stem from mental states based in passionate attachment or craving, aversion or hatred, and delusion (a lack of understanding of the true nature of existence) are considered unskilful. Those that stem from generosity and contentment, love and compassion, and wisdom are skilful. Through meditation, communication, and introspective thought, we come to see ever more clearly when we are being skilful and when we are being unskilful. Moreover, as we come to recognize more fully the harm we bring upon ourselves and others when we indulge in and act from negative mental states – and, conversely, the happiness and ease we feel in ourselves and with others when we give expression to positive mental states – we become increasingly motivated to cultivate the skilful and eradicate the unskilful.

Unless we are considerably more aware and emotionally positive than is generally the case, there are likely to be numerous occasions every day when our response to people or situations is less than skilful. If we are also working on the development of metta, we will find our ethical sensitivity grows naturally and we will find ourselves wanting to become more skilful in our interactions. It is a very good sign when people in a community start relating more in terms of ethical practice and there is a willingness to swallow one's pride and say sorry when you have said something hurtful, for example. Without this willingness to take responsibility for how our behaviour affects others or practise mutual forgiveness, a community will not get very far as a community. Bringing to mind how the Anuruddhas lived in mutual love and helpfulness may encourage us in our efforts, for they point to what is possible.

When we live in close proximity to other people, our behaviour has a very direct effect on them. If, for example, we storm through the house in a rage, our housemates would have to be very thick-skinned not to feel affected in some way. When negative emotions are strongly expressed in a community without any awareness of the other people around, they tend to have an unsettling and disturbing effect on the person themselves as well as on the general atmosphere of the community. The expression of positive emotion has the opposite effect. This doesn't mean communities should only be composed of people who experience (and express) positive emotions all the time; that is rather a tall order. Rather, everyone needs to be prepared to work on their ethics, taking seriously the Buddhist teaching that actions do indeed have consequences.

Of course, to start with, we may not always realize the connection between a particular action or non-action on our part and the observed effects. Even when we do, we may encounter some resistance to fully owning the consequences of our behaviour. Perhaps we are afraid of what others will think of us. We may fall into blaming others, or turn a blind eye to our own moral failings. Even the most confident individuals can still have areas of insecurity that may lead to avoidance tactics when it comes to taking full moral responsibility.

This is why it is so important to engender an atmosphere of genuine friendliness and kindness within a community, where we can encourage one another to become more ethical in our relations. In such an atmosphere, everyone learns to relax and trust one another more and we begin to feel how our lives are connected, part of a larger vision embodied in the values of the Three Jewels. We begin to feel that essentially everyone is trying to do the same thing and that we don't need to pull away from one another or try to prove we are better than someone else. In the larger scale of things, everyone has a lot to learn and we need as much help as we can get, so there is no point in taking the moral high ground when someone else in the community comes from less than their best. One should try to understand what led them to behave in such a way and do our best to maintain a friendly attitude towards them. After all, roles may well be reversed tomorrow.

Communities are training grounds for becoming fully responsible individuals, and it is all the small, everyday events of communal living that reveal just how mature or immature we are as a human being, let alone a spiritual being. We are being continually mirrored back by the situation, not because our failings are being pointed out by others but because through living closely with others we begin to see more clearly how our behaviour affects other people. Sometimes this can be distinctly uncomfortable. When we live on our own, it is more difficult to see our selfishness, for example, or our need to keep our world under control. I don't want to suggest that living on one's own necessarily feeds selfishness or means we are something of a control freak. Rather, living with others is more likely to show up such tendencies more quickly if they are present.

An Example

Let's take a concrete example of one of those everyday events in a community where we are faced with an ethical choice. A fairly typical situation – where we can learn quite a bit about ourselves and how far we have come (or not) in our ability to put into practice all the noble sentiments we espouse.

The example is clearing up after a meal. Okay, so the dishes need to be washed. Perhaps you have just had a meal with your fellow community members and you've been sitting on together afterwards, enjoying a stimulating conversation with one another. The conversation gradually winds down and your mind turns to what you will be doing next. Then you become aware that there are all those dishes that need washing. You are also aware that you haven't done much clearing up recently so it's probably about time you took a turn at doing it. But oh, how you hate washing the dishes. It's so boring. Given half a chance, you'll avoid it like the plague. Although your attitude does need some looking at, it need not be a particularly pressing area to work on just now. It may be that there are other practical tasks in the community that you are only too happy to do and there may happen to be plenty of other people around who enjoy washing dishes. But let's say it's not like that. No one is particularly keen on doing them. In that case you are all in the same boat and everyone needs to make the effort to go beyond their personal inclination – which is to walk away from the pile of dishes in the sink. How does one do this? Do we simply have to grit our teeth and get on with it, but with such bad grace that we almost force other people to take over doing it themselves just to improve the atmosphere? No, that isn't the answer, of course. So how do we bring a positive emotional response to our experience? What in fact is our experience when we see the dishes?

If we analyse our experience closely, perhaps we will come to see that essentially what has happened is that our eyes have made contact with the dishes. In dependence upon this contact, an unpleasant feeling tone has arisen in our mind. So what next? The blind, unaware human response is to react with aversion to unpleasant feelings, with an inconsistent, indifferent response to neutral feelings, and with craving to pleasant feelings. Here we are, facing the dishes. The sight of them evokes an unpleasant feeling in us. Then we want to remove ourselves from this apparent source of unpleasant feeling. You will notice I say 'apparent source', since the dirty dishes are of course simply dirty dishes; they are not in themselves either pleasant or unpleasant.

We now experience a definite mental state of aversion and, probably more or less concurrently, an urge to get on with something else. What that something else is may or may not be very clearly conceived in our mind. We get up and make our departure, leaving someone else to deal with the dishes. At that point, we have made an ethical choice; unfortunately, in this instance, the choice is an unethical one, based as it is in aversion. Basically, we don't care; we're behaving in a self-referential manner. At that point, when we turn our back on the dishes, we are in effect turning our back on those we live with and our vision of sharing ourselves. We're drawing a line between sharing the ideas (of ethical behaviour) that we might have been only too happily discussing in the after-dinner conversation, and sharing the chores (those ideas in practice). The other scenario (of washing the dishes, but with a bad grace) is equally unethical, as we are still essentially reacting with aversion to our experience.

Small is Big in Ethics

You might be thinking as you read this that I am stretching things a bit far and reading greater significance into this everyday occurrence than is really there. But while in itself it is a small thing, our life is made up of lots of these small, discrete instances. If we so chose, every moment of our life could be analysed in this way, and if we were to do that, we would find the pattern I have described.

Firstly, there is contact between someone or something (a 'sense object') and us (a 'sense organ' such as our eye or our ear). Then there is a feeling. Then there is a response to that feeling. This is the pattern of our lives. Our response tends to be formed by habit, therefore it will be what we may describe as 'reactive'. We need the light of greater awareness in order to have a moment of choice before we kick in with our habitual response and see what can lie between feeling and what arises next.

The Buddha encouraged his disciples to develop awareness of the mind working in this way. It is these patterns that make us the sort of person we are, as they arise, moment by moment. It is the transformation of these patterns into new, more creative responses that change us in our moment-to-moment arising.

I still haven't answered the question, though, of how to respond positively or ethically to the fact that the dishes still need to be washed despite those unpleasant feelings. But feelings don't last; they are temporary and fleeting; we don't have to build on them in the way I described. Again, we need to examine this in our own experience.

We can shift the focus of our attention and bring to mind our purpose of living with others, our sense of connection with these other people, and, by extension, our connection with all the aspects of our lives together. Suddenly, what seemed like an unpleasant chore becomes another way of being together, of showing our care for one another. You make the decision to act, to do the deed, and maybe take it as an opportunity to engage with another community member, inviting them to help you with the dishes. The task ceases to be a chore that no one feels like doing and becomes an opportunity to engage in a common task together. If we use our imagination, there is always a more creative way to deal with a situation.

Pride

A little earlier, I referred to swallowing one's pride. I am using pride in the sense of our self-view, our image of ourselves, our ego. We all have a sense of self, a view of ourselves in relation to others. Up to a point, it is a good and healthy thing to have a sense of who we are, an identity. Indeed, it is very difficult to function in the world without a coherent sense of self. However, from the standpoint of spiritual practice within the Buddhist tradition, we need to understand that this self-view will end up limiting us if we hold on to our idea of who we are too rigidly. Sometimes, for example, the reason we find it so hard to acknowledge our failings and apologize when we have said an unkind word is due to our fixed self-view, our pride. Perhaps we like to think of ourselves as perfect, or think that this is what other people expect of us. Therefore, when we experience ourselves as having been less than perfect, we try to hide this from ourselves or from others. To make an apology will challenge our misguided and fixed view of ourselves.

Something I began to notice after living in communities was that the longer I put off saying sorry after an event, the more difficult it became. I think this is because we become more fixed in our position, which in effect means fixed in our self-view. On the other hand, if our pride is strong (as has been the case with me), it may take a while to encourage ourselves to swallow our pride and loosen up around this fixing tendency. We have to be honest here about whether we are in 'putting off' mode or 'building up to positive action' mode.

Another thing I became aware of is that sometimes, in the build-up to making an apology or admitting I had been in the wrong, there was the feeling that I would lose something in the process. In a manner of speaking, I did lose something. What I lost, at least a little in that moment of apology, was the wrong view that I was perfect or ought to be perfect. A small dent was made in the tendency to fix myself as a particular sort of person. And the consequence of apologizing was an almost immediate sense of relief. It's exhausting trying to hold on to a particular view of ourselves in the face of very obvious evidence to the contrary, so it comes as a relief when we begin to let go of it. We can feel the edges of our ego softening and we discover that, rather than feel lessened, we are enriched. This isn't just to do with what happens in us; it is also to do with bringing ourselves back into deeper relationship with the other person as a friend, or potential friend, rather than holding ourselves apart from them in a slightly adversarial stance. We start realigning ourselves with how things are – namely, that we are interconnected and that we do affect one another.

Surrender: the Challenge and the Joy

Living with others isn't easy. For many of us, it offers us both the greatest challenge and the greatest joy. So where lies the challenge? And is there a connection between the challenge and the joy? Putting it briefly, the challenge lies in our tendency to self-referentiality: always acting, speaking, and thinking with the core reference being ourselves. The joy lies in overcoming this. Let's try to understand this first by looking back at the Anuruddhas.

When the Buddha asks the Anuruddhas how it is that they are living together on such friendly and harmonious terms, 'as milk and water blend, regarding one another with the eye of affection', all three of them reply in the following way.

> 'As to this, revered sir, it occurred to me: "Indeed it is a gain for me, indeed it is well gotten by me, that I am living with such fellow Brahma-farers." On account of this, revered sir, for these venerable ones friendliness as to acts of body ... acts of speech ... acts of thought, whether openly or in private, has risen up in me. Because of this, revered sir, it occurred to me: "Now, suppose that I, having surrendered my own mind, should live only according to the mind of these venerable ones?" So I, revered sir, having surrendered my own mind, am living only according to the mind of these venerable ones. Revered sir, we have divers bodies, but assuredly only one mind.
>
> 'Thus it is that we, revered sir, are living all together on friendly terms and harmoniously, as milk and water blend, regarding one another with the eye of affection.'[7]

We may notice there is a progression in what they say. First, they appreciate the opportunity to live with one another. From this naturally follows friendliness towards one another, whether in private or in public, in terms of actions of body, speech, and mind. And then, because of this friendliness that has risen up in them, a further thought or wish arises to surrender their own mind and live according to the mind of one another. Thus, they live together in a friendly and harmonious manner.

Let's look at this surrendering of one's mind to another. On the face of it, it might sound a rather dangerous and undesirable thing to do. The other translation of the story makes it a little clearer what they are pointing to here. We are told:

> 'I consider: "Why should I not set aside what I wish to do and do what these venerable ones wish to do?" Then I set aside what I wish to do and do what these venerable ones wish to do. We are different in body, venerable sir, but one in mind.'
>
> The venerable Nandiya and the venerable Kimbila each spoke likewise, adding: 'That is how, venerable sir, we are living in concord, with mutual appreciation, without disputing, blending like milk and water, viewing each other with kindly eyes.'[8]

The first thing to notice is that they each have the same attitude to one another, so it isn't a question of everyone deferring to one person, or of keeping their mouths shut through fear. There is mutuality in their wish to put aside their own wishes and follow those of another. They have worked to establish and maintain this all-round friendliness or metta towards one another 'whether openly or in private'. They love one another deeply.

As we have seen, metta expresses itself in ethical action and the willingness to work on our ethics, so we can be sure that at the stage we encounter the Anuruddhas, they have established a deep basis of trust between one another based in the mutual experience of behaving ethically towards one another.

The question arises then: with respect to *what* do they each put aside 'what I wish to do'? Would it be about anything and everything? We can take it that what they are talking about is going beyond egocentric preference. There seems to be a connection between their ability to 'set aside what I wish to do and do what these venerable ones wish to do' and their living together 'without disputing'. Many of the disputes that take place between people stem from egocentric preference. This is what the Anuruddhas were prepared to let go of in their life together. They were prepared to let go of getting their own way.

Most of us tend to view life from our own point of view rather than another's. Not only that, we tend to assume that our way of looking at things is *the* way of looking at things. This can even go as far as thinking that what suits us will suit other people, or that what we like must be what others like too. When we live with others, we begin to notice that they *don't* always seem to like the things we like. They might not like the same type of food or have the same taste in furniture or decor. They might not like pets sitting on the armchairs or beds. And they might not like getting up at six o'clock in the morning.

Building Trust

So how does one go about setting up a communal life amidst a welter of likes and dislikes? This is where we come to one of the big differences between living communally and simply sharing a house with other people but continuing to live more or less autonomously. In the latter case, each person may continue to purchase their own foodstuffs, or cook for themselves, confine any pets to their own room, and so on. To decide to live communally, we need to learn to cooperate and be willing to forgo at least some of our likes and dislikes. Indeed, we need to try to come to an altogether different way of decision-making based on genuine communication as opposed to each person speaking from their own corner, otherwise there are likely to be many petty wrangles and disputes.

It is helpful to come to a broad general agreement on various matters first. For example, will the household be vegetarian or vegan? Many practising Buddhists are intentional vegetarians out of respect for other sentient life forms. Some go a step further and become vegan. Will the wish to respect life extend to the purchase of ecologically sound cleaning products? Or recycling paper and glass? Will all food be bought communally as far as possible? The decision about the range of items purchased will need to be based on some of the above considerations as well as other factors. With good will, it is possible to come to an agreement that allows for some diversity of taste while aiming at the highest degree of communality.

Deciding on the colour scheme in a community can be an interesting exercise in cooperation and trust and could serve as an example. I have seen some successful and not so successful attempts here. The risk is that in the attempt to involve everyone, one ends up with a hotchpotch of styles and colours which in the final analysis no one likes. Or the decision-making process drags on for months on end. One of the simplest approaches, in my view, is to give the power of decision – perhaps with some level of consultation – to just one or two people.

Depending on the size of the community, there may be several areas where decisions have to be made that will impinge on the whole community: from deciding what type of washing machine to purchase when the old one breaks down to what to do with the garden. If everyone is prepared to practise in the spirit of the Anuruddhas, setting aside what they wish to do for what another wishes to do, then one can divide different areas of responsibility and decision-making between them. In this way, matters can be decided relatively easily and smoothly without cumbersome discussions involving everyone. What I realized at one stage in living with others was that it was a waste of energy on my part to try to be involved in every decision. This freed me up from having to think about a whole range of small matters. I could happily leave them to other people.

One has to make clear what matters really *do* need to involve everyone and then aim to devolve all the rest to individual community members. This takes quite a bit of trust, though. For many people, their home is where they want to feel safe and secure and in control. But communities aren't like homes in that sense. Sure, we want to feel relaxed and enjoy living there, but by its nature, community life is not about pandering to our insecurities. Through insecurity, we tend to identify strongly with our particular point of view. Through insecurity, we tend to identify with our likes and dislikes. What we need to do is turn this self-referentiality inside out and think much more in terms of considering other people's points of view. Moreover, we need to think much more in terms of genuine needs rather then in terms of passing desires. This applies with regard to both ourselves and others. If everyone in a community is working in this spirit, then our needs will be taken into account as much as somebody else's and we have nothing to fear. Surrendering to another's wishes can only happen in a healthy way on the basis of mutual love and friendliness – and mutual consideration. This means everyone needs to be engaged in the cultivation of metta and work on their own ethical practice.

One doesn't get any sense of the Anuruddhas feeling hard done by or disadvantaged through their decision to forgo egocentric preferences. On the contrary, it is a contributory factor to why they are able to live in harmony, without disputes; and surely that must be a very enjoyable thing. Disharmony is painful. There is something very beautiful in harmony. With their sights set on a common higher purpose – total liberation or Enlightenment – the Anuruddhas are only too happy to let go of egocentric preferences, knowing that in so doing they will move more rapidly towards their goal.

A Beautiful Whole

Harmony has to be worked at. Sometimes people can think harmony means keeping the peace, or trying to iron out the differences between people. But this is not so. Harmony recognizes the differences between people – differences of approach and temperament, for example. Musicians in an orchestra manage with effort to blend all the sounds from the different musical instruments into a single harmonious whole. Similarly, if we keep bearing in mind the overall purpose for which we are living together in a community – namely to support one another's spiritual aspirations – this will help motivate us to work at coming to a deeper mutual understanding.

Deepening mutual understanding conduces to harmony. However, to understand another person deeply takes time. Although we share what is most essential – the human condition with its possibility of spiritual liberation – we are, in another sense, all unique and quite different one from another. This needs to be taken into account when we communicate. We need to be interested in one another and prepared to take each other in fully. Amongst other things, this involves looking at the other person when they are speaking and really taking in what they are saying or trying to say. Very often we are only half listening and jump to premature conclusions. We need to learn to ask questions too. It is only too easy to assume we know what someone is talking about because they seem to be speaking the same language, yet this is often exactly where misunderstandings come in. We use the same language in different ways and unless we are very precise in our communication, there is plenty of room for interpretation. Even when we are very clear, unless we are dealing with simple, verifiable, objective facts, there is still scope for misunderstanding as we all tend to filter what others say through our own way of understanding things. It may help to bear in mind a little aphorism by my spiritual teacher: 'Don't argue, discuss.'[9]

When misunderstandings or arguments do occur we need to get ourselves back in communication with the other person or persons through willingness to take responsibility for any part we might have played. This begins to transform disharmony into harmony; indeed, it often brings a deeper level of harmony because we have to come to a deeper understanding of what went wrong and why. This may tell us something new about the other person and ourselves. This growth in understanding will then flow on into subsequent interactions.

A couple more images spring to mind, which are suggestive of the nature of the harmony we are looking to cultivate in community. Life with others is like the play of colours in a kaleidoscope. As you turn the kaleidoscope, all the pieces of coloured glass or plastic shift their position and create yet another new and beautiful pattern. Similarly, each interaction in a community contributes to the overall atmosphere and character of the community. When the kaleidoscope initially turns, the variously coloured pieces of glass start moving, the old pattern dissolves, and it's not clear what will appear next. So, too, in communication there is an element of stepping into the unknown, of not knowing quite what is going to come out of the communication. In a sense, we have to be prepared for anything. The kaleidoscope image illustrates the fact of change in a community: it is not a static entity but a dynamic whole. Every communication subtly or not so subtly has an effect, either adding to or detracting from the development of greater understanding and harmony.

Another image is that of the mandala. A definition of a mandala by a Tibetan teacher, Rongzompo Chokyi Zangpo, is: 'To make a mandala is to take any prominent aspect of reality and surround it with beauty.' So a community might place a vision of friendship and communal harmony such as the Anuruddhas embody at the centre of the mandala. Then everyone in the community would do their best to approach all aspects of communal life in the light of that vision so that they support rather than hinder the gradual embodiment of that vision in the community. The skilful action of each person in the community in relation to the others, in the light of the common vision, is beautiful.

Of course, this beauty has to be brought into being; we are learning how to live together. In order to reach ever greater harmony we need to keep reminding ourselves of our overall purpose, the vision of what we are aiming for both individually and collectively.

4

SIMPLY SHARE

Life in a community of spiritual aspirants can be a daunting prospect. In fact, it can boil down to some very basic elements about how we choose to live our lives – together. Let's look again at the Anuruddhas to see if they can provide us with some examples.

The Buddha listens to these three young men telling him of how they live in mutual love and kindness and of their decision not to indulge in personal likes and dislikes in their shared life. The conversation continues:

'Good, it is good, Anuruddhas. But I hope that you, Anuruddhas, are living diligent, ardent, self-resolute?'

'Yes, certainly, revered sir, we are living diligent, ardent, self-resolute.'

'And how is it that you, Anuruddhas, are living diligent, ardent, self-resolute?'

'As to this, revered sir, whoever of us returns first from going to a village for almsfood makes ready a seat, sets out water for drinking and water for washing the

feet, and sets out a refuse-bowl. Whoever returns last
from going to a village for almsfood, if there are the
remains of a meal and if he so desires, he eats them; if
he does not desire to do so, he throws them out where
there are no crops, or he drops them into water where
there are no living creatures; he puts up the seat, he
puts away the water for drinking and the water for
washing, he puts away the refuse-bowl, he sweeps the
refectory. Whoever sees a vessel for drinking water or a
vessel for washing water or a vessel for water for
rinsing after evacuation, void and empty, he sets out
water. If it is impossible for him to do this by a
movement of his hand, having invited a companion to
help us by signalling to him with the hand, we set out
the water; but we do not, revered sir, for such reason,
break into speech. And then we, revered sir, once in
every five nights sit down together for talk on
dhamma. It is thus, revered sir, that we are dwelling
diligent, ardent, self-resolute.'

'Good, it is good, Anuruddhas.'[10]

The Buddha says he hopes the Anuruddhas are dwelling 'diligent, ardent, and self-resolute' and when they
confirm that they are, he invites them to elaborate on
how they are so doing. In other words, he wants to hear
something about the practical working out of the mutual love they espouse. How do they express it? In reply,
they tell him how they go about the practical chores of
living together.

It is striking just how simple their life is. There is no
house to maintain, no rent or mortgage repayments, no

bills to pay, no money needed, no cooking to do; very little, in fact, to distract them from meditation and reflection on the teachings of the Buddha. Simple though their lifestyle is compared with ours, it nevertheless brings to our attention a number of areas we can apply to a community of spiritual aspirants in the twenty-first century: simplicity of lifestyle, sharing of material resources, environmental awareness, mutual responsibility for the practical running of the household, mutual cooperation, and meaningful communication.

The Simple Life

The first three areas under consideration here are related: simplicity of lifestyle, sharing material resources, and being environmentally aware.

First, let's think about simplicity of lifestyle. Look at what we know of the Anuruddhas. There is nothing extraneous in the lifestyle of these three young men, neither material possessions nor how they use their time and energy. Everything revolves around their quest for meaning. This is important to note; they have a clear, overarching vision and sense of purpose that guides the choices they make. Their simplicity of lifestyle is one such choice.

Without an overarching vision, it is easy to get lost in the complexity of life – and life today is particularly complex; not simply because we need to live in a building rather than under a tree or have to earn a living in order to eat and have a roof over our head – although some might say that's bad enough. There are just so many pulls on our attention, so many choices and options open to us, far more than would have been the case for those young men even when they were still living a household life. There is an almost infinite range of commodities we can purchase with our money as well as innumerable things we can do with our leisure time. We can devote our time and energy to many worthy causes. We have access to many different skills. In some ways, it is wonderful to have so much choice. In another way, it's a terrible responsibility to exercise that choice wisely.

Western society today seems to require us to live materially complex lives in order to make our way in it, even as spiritual practitioners or would-be spiritual practitioners. It's important to recognize that we can still exercise a lot of choice in this respect. We have a choice in terms of how many material goods we acquire, how many labour-saving gadgets and devices we invest in, the type of property we live in, an so on. All these factors will, in turn, contribute to determining the amount of money we need to earn to support our lifestyle. We live in a consumer-driven society and we all have to work hard against the relentless efforts of the advertising industry that encourages us to buy, buy, buy. We need to develop some sense of purpose to our lives as a clearer basis from which to exercise choice wisely and develop a simplicity of lifestyle where everything is of a piece, as it were.

Where community living is concerned, there are other choices to be made, not only in material terms but also in terms of time and energy. After all, communities are not just about a bunch of people living under the same roof but leading quite separate lives. Unfortunately, they can sometimes be like that: a place where people come and go and don't impinge on each other; more like a shared house than a community. However, if we are to make a success of a community, we will need to make some choices as to where we invest our energies. We will need to have energy available to put into the community, not only practically but also in terms of communication with one another. If we have too many external pulls on our time and energy, not much is going to build up in the community, or it is going to take a long time. Of course, it may be that we have the type of job that demands us to work long hours, travel long distances, and so on. And it may be that this job is a vocation and we would not want to change it for something less demanding or more local. This needn't be an unconquerable difficulty, but if most or all of the people in the community are in a similar situation then, yes, it will take longer to build up a depth of communication. This is somewhat different, though, to a situation where people are trying to fit too many things into their lives and don't realize the effect this is having on the community.

I have mentioned a mandala as a metaphor for a community. Each person is an element in that mandala, and that means their physical and emotional presence or absence does have an effect on the rest of the community. One can also talk in terms of each member's personal mandala. Some people may have very rich and complex personal mandalas, with many interests and friends, whereas others may have very simple ones. A mix of such people in a community can work. Difficulties can and do arise, though, if some people have their main friendships outside the community and don't feel very motivated to build deeper friendships within it. Or there is the opposite scenario: some may be looking to the community to meet all their needs for personal friendship and find they're resentful that those needs aren't being met. We may or may not have many friends elsewhere by the time we move into a community, but we still need to be interested in getting to know our fellow community members and be open to entering deeper spiritual relationships with them over time. While it probably isn't feasible to develop close personal friendships with everyone we live with, through sharing a common pattern of life we will notice connections gradually building between us. We could call this a field of friendship. If we are clear about this, then over time we will naturally come to see whether our lives need simplifying in order to do justice to the communal lifestyle we have now chosen.

Single-Sex Communities
Is it significant that the Anuruddhas, our example of the essence of community living, do not live in a community comprised of men and women? Does its single-sex nature have any bearing on our discussion of simplicity of lifestyle?

These three young men are avowed celibates. This was part and parcel of the commitment made by the men and women who went forth from home into home-lessness under the Buddha's guidance. Given this fact, it is not surprising they were not living with women.[11]

In the West today, the homeless lifestyle is not recog-nized as something desirable. While many people are, indeed, homeless, this is not usually taken to be a posi-tive thing. People today usually end up in such a situ-ation through unfortunate circumstances rather than by conscious choice (though some may have adopted a homeless life through semi-conscious spiritual impulses or a deliberate wish to opt out of modern society). The freedom of the simple life enjoyed by the wandering disciples of the Buddha can be approached in different ways, however. If we feel the urge to simplify our life more radically in the light of our spiritual vision, it does not have to take the form of a literally homeless life. A community based in spiritual values is not meant to be a home as the word is generally understood – so it is certainly possible in the world of today to establish residential communities that in their own way are as radical and uncomplicated as the community the Anuruddhas created under the open skies in that forest clearing.

For example, we can choose to create a single-sex residential community – a community composed solely of men or of women. As it is a community of people drawn together primarily on the basis of a common spiritual interest rather than romantic interest, it is arguably less complicated than, and certainly radically different from, most other lifestyles. For it is probably true of most people that there is an unthinking assumption or hope that, at some point, they will live with a sexual partner, with or without the company of others.

I would like to suggest that choosing to establish or join a single-sex community can contribute to simplicity of lifestyle, but before exploring this further, I'd like to relate an experience I had many years ago. Sangharakshita, my spiritual teacher, asked me at one point to go to the United States and tour some of the Buddhist groups there, arranging particularly to meet with some of the prominent women teachers associated with those groups. This I did and, in several situations, I found myself attempting to explain why we in the FWBO encouraged the establishment of single-sex communities in preference to mixed communities. Interestingly, only two of the groups I visited conducted any single-sex activities, and in no cases were there any single-sex communities. With each new person I met, the question of 'why' arose in their minds. In each case, I found it very hard, if not impossible, to get across to people who had no experience of such communities what the benefits could be. I experimented, approaching the subject from different angles, but each time I was met with looks of incomprehension or definite reservations about such a community. It seemed to go so much against the grain of modern thinking – at least in the USA – to consider the possibility that grown men and women would benefit from living solely with other members of their own sex. I arrived at the conclusion that a single-sex lifestyle is essentially an esoteric experience. In other words, one needs to try it out and then one will find out the benefits for oneself at first hand.

However, it is certainly possible to experience these benefits of having a single-sex element in one's life well before making the decision to move into a single-sex community. For example, the FWBO offers single-sex study groups and retreats on a regular basis. This also means that anyone can avail themselves of such situations, whether or not they are in a position to live in a community.

According to Buddhist tradition, spiritual life consists, among other things, in 'a progression from a state of biological and psychological sexual dimorphism to a state of spiritual androgyny.'[12] The latter is a state in which there is no self-identification either as a a man or as a woman. It is a mode of being or experience characterized by a deep calm and contentment in which we are no longer compelled to seek satisfaction or happiness or contentment outside ourselves. This doesn't mean we no longer enjoy other people or things; if anything we can enjoy them more in a light and non-compulsive way. By contrast, the former state of biological and psychological sexual dimorphism is one in which our identity is tied up with our gender. This gender-identification affects how we relate to the world, and in particular how we relate to members of the opposite sex. There tend to be varying degrees of projection, tension, and discontent in our experience as a consequence.

Whatever our sexual orientation there is a tendency for both women and men to project on to members of the opposite sex qualities and attributes one does not recognize as present, or potentially present, in oneself. This limits who one is as a person. It can also lead to unhealthy patterns of dependence.

Living with members of our own sex naturally throws us back on ourselves to find within the qualities we usually attribute to the opposite sex. We may notice on occasion a sense of absence or lack when solely in the company of our own sex. If so, we can ask ourselves what we are missing in our experience, and whether what we feel to be missing is a positive quality or experience. If it is, where do we think such qualities or experience are to be found? The answers to these kinds of questions may not always lead us to a member of the opposite sex, but they might. If they do, we can first of all take it as a good sign that we are waking up to the fact we rely to some extent at least on being with members of the opposite sex for a sense of completeness. Once we realize this, we can begin to do something about it and, up to a point, the simple fact of living with members of our own sex will begin to draw more out of us.

Meditation will also help us move towards becoming spiritually androgynous. In deeper meditation, when we have become fully absorbed in the object of concentration (e.g. the breath or metta) all our energies are flowing together as a single harmonious whole. This is deeply satisfying as well as pleasurable. We feel content and happy. For the time being we have risen above the state of sexual dimorphism. When we conclude such a session of meditation we may notice this experience of positive containment and contentment carries on for a while through the sheer momentum of the effort we have put in. We will go on to notice how we start to fall away from that level of contentment and ease.

Living with members of our own sex supports the process of meditation – and simplification of our life – as it temporarily removes us from one of the most basic triggers for our attention and energies to start dividing and polarizing again. In a very basic and fundamental way, we are surrounded by 'like' and this helps us stay centred within ourselves. This simplifies our experience and supports our spiritual endeavours. The Anuruddhas took a further step to simplify their life and support their overall purpose by practising celibacy.

Does Single-Sex Mean No Sex?

Do sexual relations fit anywhere in all this? Many of us are not yet ready to 'go forth' to the extent of embracing celibacy as a way of life. A single-sex community doesn't preclude one's being sexually active – whatever one's sexual orientation. Broadly speaking, though, in choosing to live communally, we need to be prepared to revise our views on the place of a sexual relationship in our life. There are no hard-and-fast rules in this respect. Each person has to work this out for themselves in the context of the particular community of people they have chosen to live with. But it is important to recognize that living with others communally is something that we learn how to do through practice – and by learning from the example of others more experienced than ourselves in community living.

We need to be aware, however, that, in the usual run of things, sexual relations tend to take up a great deal of time and emotional energy. A community is essentially about people. We are particularly interested here in looking at communities where people have chosen to live together in order to consciously support each other in leading the spiritual life. To support one another in this way, we need to get to know one another. If most of our attention lies outside the community with a sexual partner, we will not readily develop deeper relationships with those we live with. If several people in the community are in a similar position, the community will not have much life in it and will be somewhat limited as a context that supports spiritual growth. It isn't just a question of how much time we spend with our partner, it is also a question of where our emotional centre lies. It is easy to fool oneself in this area. It is possible, for example, not to see our partner very often but still to be somewhat emotionally absent or unavailable to those we are living with. If we aren't prepared to put much of ourselves into a community, we aren't likely to gain much either.

To conclude, then, that the young men of our story live in a single-sex situation is significant. It is an important component in the simplicity of their lifestyle that also supports their overall spiritual purpose. To live in an environment that does not stimulate or encourage gender-polarization makes things less complicated. It makes things clearer. It frees up energy that would otherwise be lost in such projections and encourages us to plough it back into deepening our spiritual practice – and our relationships with others. This process is further encouraged by the practice of celibacy.

Simplifying one's life is an important element in developing a community – and in the spiritual life in general. However, how we move towards greater simplicity is a process that each individual needs to work out for themselves; the results will be greater energy and focus within the community that can be of benefit to all its members.

Sharing Material Resources

Whether we attach great or little importance to them, we all have to make choices on the material level, and this is a very interesting area to examine. Through living together with others, we can pool our material and economic resources and live more simply. How far we take this is up to us, but it has potentially far-reaching implications.

The Anuruddhas more or less hold everything in common. While they collect their own food from the local villagers, they share what they don't need. They also share any other small items used in the running of their simple household: buckets, broom, seats, and so on. The fact they have very few possessions between them might lead us to underestimate the significance of this simplicity and sharing. However, we know from other incidents recorded from the time of the Buddha that some of his homeless disciples were discovered to be taking advantage of the householders' generosity and beginning to stockpile gifts of cloth and so on. Clearly, learning to share and not accumulate material things is a practice (and can take practice), however little you have.

We have seen that in the West today our lives are much more materially complex, with ever-increasing consumerism as the norm. Going against that trend is not easy, but living with others can help us make choices about what we acquire and where we spend our money. It gives us an opportunity to experiment in this area of our life and find out how much money we really need to live comfortably yet simply. It's about meeting our real needs as opposed to our potentially infinite yet often arbitrary desires.

How much do we really need to call our own? In community, we have more opportunity to pool our resources and reappraise our attitude to ownership. For instance, we will need only one set of most household items, such as a fridge, cooker, crockery, washing machine, furniture, and perhaps even a television and a car. It might be that the founding community members purchase all such items and hold them in common, with the understanding that they belong to the community rather than to any one individual or set of individuals. In this case, unless the community disbands completely, these items are likely to stay on as resources for future community members even when some of the original community members leave. The community may decide to give some of these items to the person who is leaving to help them set up home elsewhere and then reinvest in more goods for the community. This approach reflects common ownership of these material goods.

We can have as a practice taking care of those things we own in common, being careful not to squander our collective resources through treating things carelessly so that they have to be replaced more frequently than necessary. Unfortunately, something that can happen in communities is that things held in common are not as well cared for as those owned personally. We need to learn to take care of things we do not personally own, whether they are held in common or lent to us by another community member. People do have different standards in this respect and this can sometimes lead to difficulties. For some people, to dog-ear a book or leave it stained with tea or coffee is of no consequence. For another, such treatment almost borders on sacrilege. In either case, it is important to cultivate respect for other people's property and treat it as well as they would themselves, or even better. A community has to try to arrive at some generally agreed standards of care and consideration where things held in common or used in common are involved.

Another scenario is that some items, whilst being used in common, are owned by individuals. Perhaps somebody moves into the community with a fridge or cooker and is happy for the community to use that item as long as they live there. When they leave, though, so too will those items unless the person decides to donate them to the community. This situation reflects shared use rather than common ownership.

A more profound practice is that of sharing where there is no sense of personal ownership at all. We have gone beyond sharing the use of something that we still relate to as fundamentally ours. This takes a lot of courage and confidence and is most likely to start with the sharing of just a few things between close friends where there is a lot of mutual love and trust. Perhaps we begin to share books or tapes, maybe clothes or a car. Eventually, we may share everything, even earnings, and not just with one person but with several. As with so many aspects of spiritual practice, this is a gradual path. It is not realistic to think we can move from a sense of personal ownership to no sense of ownership in one go. Learning to share the use of our things more readily is likely to be our main working ground in this area for some time. However, as deepening mutual trust and love develops, we may find that we naturally start moving little by little in the direction of this profounder level of sharing.

When the Anuruddhas speak to the Buddha of their relationship with one another, they say: 'Revered sir, we have divers bodies, but assuredly only one mind.' In other words, they feel themselves to be united on a deep spiritual level. They see themselves to be essentially 'as one' in the sense of having transcended the distinction between self and other. When this has become our abiding experience we can't help but share everything, for we don't feel any difference between ourselves and others. Usually we experience property as an extension of ourselves, but when that seemingly irreconcilable difference between self and other breaks down, so too does any sense of personal ownership. It is a very beautiful vision that cuts right across the ways of the modern world, for the concept of ownership has run riot with every inch of land, every creation, even every idea, being apportioned and labelled as belonging to someone or to some corporate body or state.

It is a beautiful and lofty vision. We will be making a good start if we are able to share our things more, becoming increasingly generous with the material resources that we have at our disposal.

Caring for the Environment

This brings me on to the third related area: being environmentally aware. This is a big subject and much has been written on it. I can do little more than flag it as an area that warrants our serious consideration if it hasn't done already. The Anuruddhas speak of disposing of any unwanted remains of a meal where there are no crops, or dropping them into water where there are no living creatures. Of course, we now know that water will have microbes in it, if nothing else, but the point is that, to the best of their knowledge, they acted in such a way as to cause the least damage to their environment, including other life forms. We can but try to do likewise.

Non-violence is an important dimension of spiritual practice within the Buddhist tradition. To live in a way that causes the least amount of harm to other life forms and the planet as a whole, as well as to actively cultivate love and compassion towards all beings, is in accordance with this principle. Perhaps the single most significant step we can take in this area is to become a vegan or at least a vegetarian.

Not wasting the food and energy resources of the planet is one more dimension of practice. Communal living doesn't necessarily mean we use less resources per capita than a single person living on their own, but it is an opportunity to do so. How many televisions or cars do we need altogether? How many rooms do we really need individually? How much convenience food do we have to consume? Another dimension is to consider using environmentally-friendly cleaning products, toiletries, and so on which break down easily, as well as to consider the benefits of recycling paper, tins, glass, and plastics where possible. In the end, we need to come to see the connection between living more simply and conserving energy (and to see that these are in line with Buddhist principles) in order to be motivated to act with environmental awareness.

Mutual Responsibility and Cooperation

I touched earlier on mutual responsibility as a necessary component of community living. Let's briefly revisit it. The Anuruddhas all chip in and help with the communal chores. It is hard to know from their brief account whether they simply see what needs to be done for the smooth running of the household and get on with it spontaneously or whether they are following some agreed system. It is possible that they decided after some discussion to follow a particular system in terms of mealtimes, for they seem to have clearly delineated tasks depending on who returns first or last from the almsround. On the other hand, when it comes to keeping the various water vessels filled, it is a question of who first notices they have become empty. That person refills them, silently signalling one of the others for help if necessary. Overall, there is no question of them having to be told what to do or of being taken to task for not pulling their weight. Clearly, they have come to a common agreement on how to live together and happily do so. This is what we need to do when living with others.

There are numerous practical areas involved in living together, and each community needs to decide how best to meet those needs. Will there be any communal meals and, if so, at what time? Will there be rotas for cleaning, cooking, and shopping? Who will pay the bills and how will costs be apportioned? You might need to experiment a bit to see what works best for all concerned. Small communities of two or three people shouldn't need as much, if any, structuring in terms of rotas, compared to larger communities of five or more where a certain amount of coordination is necessary. Whatever systems we create, we need to maintain flexibility in order to be able to respond spontaneously when more help is required or when an unforeseen need arises. It's best to guard against sticking rigidly to our area, abiding by the letter of the system but forgetting the spirit of mutual care and responsibility and cooperation we are aiming to engender between us. Let's keep in mind that our practical duties follow from our wish to live with fellow spiritual aspirants and that the way we go about them is a concrete way of expressing our love and care for one another.

Sometimes people have the mistaken idea that spiritual practice is essentially concerned with meditation. This can lead to the creation of an artificial distinction between what one regards as spiritual – here, meditation – and the rest of one's life. Consequently, one can tend to be rather blinkered in one's approach to spiritual practice. One can be mainly concerned about how one is doing in meditation, not paying sufficient regard to how one is in the rest of one's life, which for most people will constitute the greater part of their time. In fact, spiritual practice concerns *all* areas. Every situation is an opportunity to deepen our understanding and awareness of ourselves and others. Each situation is an opportunity to act from love, from metta, rather than from aversion or disinterest. So, in a community, our communal duties are opportunities for spiritual practice. They are not something tedious and boring which we have to get out of the way as quickly as possible so we can get on with more 'interesting' or 'exciting' aspects of our practice.

Meaningful Communication

On reading of the story of the Anuruddhas, we might think meaningful communication doesn't play a large part in community living because of the degree of silence they observed. (They only spoke together every fifth night.) However, that isn't necessarily the case for all communities or, indeed, for very many. To begin with, the Anuruddhas lived mostly in silence because they had chosen to follow a meditative lifestyle. Trying to combine a lot of meditation with a lot of talking doesn't work very well, which is why, within the Buddhist tradition, intensive meditation retreats are generally conducted almost entirely in silence. Unless a community is predominantly a meditative community, the balance of silence and verbal communication will be very different to that of the Anuruddhas' community because it will have quite different needs.

Secondly, meaningful communication doesn't necessarily have to mean a lot of *verbal* communication. We get the impression that the Anuruddhas were in meaningful communication not just on the evenings when they discussed the Dharma. We have seen how responsive they were to one another, helping each other run their simple household. We have heard how deep was their love for one another. So despite the lack of verbal communication, there was a high degree of mutual awareness and care expressed between them. Even if we are unlikely to live in a community that observes as much silence as the Anuruddhas, there is still plenty of scope to develop meaningful non-verbal communication.

For example, we can show care for those we live with in numerous small ways that do not involve verbal speech. We can put some flowers or a card of welcome in another's room on their return from a trip away, water their plants when they go on retreat, or bring washing in from the line if it starts to rain. We could help carry their luggage down the stairs, smile as you pass in the hall, put your arm round someone's shoulder when they look a bit down, or give them a hug, and so on.

A little later, we'll look at the place of silence in communities. For now, let's consider what makes verbal communication meaningful from a Buddhist perspective. We can still draw on the Anuruddhas as the jumping-off point for our discussion because the degree and type of verbal communication that they did have points to two underlying principles of communication. Those two principles are conservation of energy, particularly psychical energy for the task in hand, and, not unrelated, the appropriate use of energy.

Speech involves energy. It is an outpouring of psychical energy, mental-cum-emotional energy expressed in speech. In the extended set of ethical precepts that I follow (extended, that is, from a set of five generally taken by all those who consider themselves to be practising Buddhists, to ten),[13] there are no less than four speech precepts, which draws our attention to what an important area of practice this is. These precepts identify four key areas we need to watch for and abstain from in terms of energy leakage: false speech, harsh speech, useless or frivolous speech, and slanderous speech. The positive counterparts of these tendencies are the types of speech we need to cultivate that will channel and conserve energy as well as stimulate and encourage healthy energy flow. These are truthful speech, kindly and gracious speech, helpful speech, and harmonious speech. Depending on the type of communication we are engaged in, speech may be either energizing or draining. Speech releases and stimulates energy when we engage in meaningful communication with another human being, but when we indulge in verbal negativity or listen at length to another's, we are likely to end up feeling emotionally drained. Less obviously harmful, but no less wasteful of energy, is getting carried away, wasting energy in excessive frivolity. Sometimes such frivolity can be a way of avoiding issues that need to be addressed. Not that our communication has to be deadly serious; good-humoured playfulness can be a meaningful way of engaging with others and has its place.

Speech, communication, is a powerful tool for transformation. We all know this from our own experience. We are affected by our conversations with people; they change us. Our mental states change as a result of our conversations; sometimes they improve and become more positive, sometimes they deteriorate and become more negative. As with everything, we have a choice and we need to learn to take increasing responsibility for the consequences of our actions of speech, for speech is an action. Contrary to the saying 'sticks and stones may break my bones but words can never hurt me,' an

Eastern proverb goes, 'Sticks and stones may break one's bones but speech can cut out a heart.' This proverb reflects greater wisdom. The converse of this idea is that the power of speech, the deepening communication with those who share the same spiritual values, can help us to grow spiritually. It is our common interest in, even love of, those values that increasingly needs to inform our speech with one another. This will make our speech with each other meaningful.

Apart from all the spontaneous opportunities for communication with each other that arise in a community, we may also choose to have regular community meetings. We may have community evenings and/or community days. We may even go away together for a weekend. On such occasions, we may choose to discuss specific themes, such as our practice of the ethical precepts or our meditation, or we may study the Dharma together. Telling our life stories can be a good way to build a basis of sympathy and understanding in a community where people do not know each other very well. Sharing our reflections on current sources of inspiration and interest from the world of art or literature or music can be another fruitful means of engaging with one another's lives in a meaningful way. Simply being prepared to discuss what is currently on our mind is very helpful. To talk about our concerns and preoccupations as well as our interests will help to involve those we live with more in our life and provides openings for mutual learning and growth.

All experience is the raw material for spiritual transformation; there is nothing that is not relevant or does not need eventually to be brought into the light of Truth. There is no event that is not an occasion for learning. This being so, we are, in communication, entering upon a potentially rich field of mutual exploration. Living with others in community, we come face to face with their joys and sorrows, struggles and successes. If we are really prepared to enter into communication with our fellow community members, we will discover many new things, both in them and in ourselves. Our thinking will be put to the test, our ideas on all manner of things modified or radically altered through the introduction of new ideas and perspectives. Our range of feeling and sympathy will be enlarged, more will be drawn out of us, and we will gradually learn what it means to put the Dharma into practice.

Let the Silence Speak

How does silence play a role in this important feature, meaningful communication? I have already touched on a few of the ways we can give non-verbal expression to our care and concern for those with whom we live. Even simply being together in silence is a form of communication; it is not simply an absence of sound. The Anuruddhas remained in silence together most of the time, as this was most conducive to a lot of meditation. Clearly they felt completely at ease being together like this and were very in tune with one another. While our lifestyle may not require the 'support' of silence to the degree the Anuruddhas' did, there will still be benefits to having some experience of silence in a community. Strange as it may seem, if we are able to relax into silence with others, this can lead to a deeper level of mutual awareness and sympathy.

For most of us, silence is a practice. Many people might not feel that comfortable being in silence with others; they may feel it to be something of a punishment or something they have to endure. I remember one community I lived in where at some stage we experimented with introducing silent meals. It didn't work very well. Some people felt distinctly uncomfortable, and others, like me, felt uneasy about others' discomfort, with the result that there was an awkward tension in the atmosphere that wasn't a good basis for enjoying or digesting one's food. The experiment was dropped. These days, I regularly eat dinner in silence both in my own community and at a neighbouring community that has a similar custom. In the main, I enjoy it or, let's say, I enjoy it when I manage to be fully present and relaxed. On retreat, I find it much easier to eat silently with others in a relaxed way, mainly because my mind has calmed down and is less busy with thoughts about this and that. At home, if I have come straight from work, I can still be thinking about all sorts of things. In this case, although I am abstaining from speech, I am only minimally aware either of what I am eating or of my companions. Then it is a definite practice to calm my mind and try to become more present in the situation. In the past, the whole process outside of a retreat context felt too much like an ordeal. I don't feel that nowadays. I am happy to work with the silence as a practice and actually prefer to eat quietly and fall into conversation afterwards.

I recently had a short holiday with a good friend. When we arrived at our destination, we discovered that we were booked into a rather small room with almost all the available floor space taken up with two beds, a table, chairs, and wardrobe. It was a situation where either of us could have become a bit tense, given our respective tendencies. Actually, I was struck by how easy it was for us to slip in and out of silence together over those few days in a relaxed way. We were able to drop into our own worlds yet stay connected. I took it as a good sign in terms of our friendship that we could be like this with each other.

It isn't very easy to be in silence with others if we are not even that comfortable being in silence on our own. These days, many people seem to deliberately live with almost continual background noise from the moment they wake up to the moment they turn out the light and go to bed with noise from the radio, stereo, television, or whatever. This is rather different from the noise of the jungle that the Anuruddhas would have had! We could start by experimenting in living without a background of such noise.

Our first taste of a fuller silence, silence as a practice in a Buddhist context, might occur on a retreat. Short periods of silence are often introduced as a support to meditation and to help us assimilate what is happening to us. It can come as quite a relief to drop into silence at such times and to discover that we can still engage with others. Absence of speech doesn't have to mean absence of communication. Indeed, we may take in another person more fully in silence. Sometimes words get in the way. As we get over any awkwardness or embarrassment we may feel, a new dimension of communication opens up which is quite beautiful. A community could build up to more formal periods of silence, as a *natural* evolution of communication between people. It's not something to rush into when you hardly know one another. Probably the most common situations into which to introduce silence in a community are around mealtimes or in the morning before or around a period of meditation.

5

BEAUTY INSIDE AND OUT

Meditation

I have mentioned meditation more than once in looking at community living and, particularly, living in Buddhist communities. I introduced the Metta Bhavana meditation practice earlier on when we were looking at the importance of love and friendliness as a basis of living with others. So let's look more closely at meditation.

Close, eyes; behold no more the rich array
Of forms and vivid colours. Touch, be still;
Grope not for lover's hand, or lips that will
Sting you awake to bliss by night or day.
Relish no more the scent of new-mown hay,
Or flowers, or incense, nostrils. Take your fill
Of tastes no more, O watery tongue, nor trill
Delicious notes in cadence grave or gay.

For when the senses and the sensual mind
Are laid asleep, and self itself suspended,

And naught is left to strive for or to seek,
Then, to the inmost spirit, thrice refined,
Thrice pure, before that trance sublime has ended,
With voice of thunder, will the Silence speak.[14]

The Anuruddhas live in a meditation community. Meditation is their principal activity. However, this isn't the only type of community one can have. After all, to live a full-time meditative life isn't going to be to everyone's taste, or even possible for everyone. Sometimes, though, when one has just come home from a very positive experience on retreat, one might fantasize that it could be. The majority of communities in the Buddhist movement I am involved with are city-based and most of the members of these various communities all hold full-time or part-time jobs. Most, if not all, of the men and women who live in those communities meditate daily, or at least fairly regularly.

The Buddhist path is concerned with transformation of the way we relate to the world and the way we conduct ourselves within it. It involves transformation of our mind. 'Mind' here means not only the cognitive dimension, but also the emotional and volitional dimensions. Meditation is a direct means of working on our minds.

In living together with other spiritual practitioners or would-be practitioners, we are aiming to help one another mutually explore and bring alive, individually and collectively, the values in which we most deeply believe, as embodied in the Three Jewels. Meditation is a primary method for doing this, alongside other areas of practice, some of which we have already explored. It is not surprising, then, that meditation should feature in community life. If everyone in the community is meditating regularly, it will not only help each person individually to raise their level of consciousness, but also enhance the level of communication of the whole community.

It isn't easy to establish a daily meditation practice, for reasons mentioned earlier. For many of us, living with people who also meditate helps us to keep making the effort ourselves. In my first community, we didn't meditate together, but just *knowing* that others were doing so in their own rooms was supportive. It wasn't until my fourth community that I found myself in a situation where we set aside a room in the house specially for meditation and had a set time each morning when we would come together to meditate. This was even more supportive and enriching than meditating separately. You can set up a communal meditation practice using a lounge or someone's bedroom. However, if you can afford to give over one room in the house to meditation, so much the better. For it can be helpful to have a clear, uncluttered space in which to meditate, free from associations with other activities such as work, eating, talking, sleeping, and so on. Over time, as more and more meditation takes place in the room, and possibly devotional practices too, a tangible atmosphere builds up that can support our efforts to concentrate and still the mind.

With a communal meditation practice, we become more visible to each other. This can encourage even greater efforts on the part of each person to overcome the resistances that inevitably arise to getting up each day to meditate before work. Also, we share a form of communication with our fellow community members when we meet in this way, which we may not otherwise do. In other words, it is silence as a form of communication. Moreover, if we meet like this and do some devotional practice together beforehand, such as reciting the Three Refuges and the ethical precepts we are endeavouring to practise, this has a strong orienting effect on the community. We set the scene every day for the basis of our individual and collective practice.

We have already seen in the section on simplicity of lifestyle that meditation in the sense of absorption is a deeply satisfying experience. In order to become so absorbed we need to rise above certain mental-cum-emotional hindrances (the same ones the Anuruddhas struggled with in the earlier stage of their spiritual lives): craving for sensual experience, aversion, doubt, restlessness and anxiety, sloth and torpor. An unpleasant bunch! These tendencies of mind also play themselves out in everyday life when we behave unskilfully. Working on the ethical dimension of our practice in the community will support our efforts to concentrate our minds in meditation. And the positive mental states we come to experience through becoming absorbed will feed in to our relationships within the community.

Meditation and community living can support more far-reaching changes in us, though. I've spoken of how both can support the cultivation and prolongation of androgynous states of mind. From a Buddhist point of view, the polarization and projection between the sexes is but a marked and vivid example of the general existential state of polarization between so-called 'subject' and so-called 'object' from which all unenlightened beings suffer all the time. ('Subject' here means that which we commonly think of as 'me', and 'object' that which we commonly think of as 'not me' or 'other'.) Enlightened beings, by contrast, have transcended all these modes of dualistic thinking and outlook.

Meditation (and indeed the whole spiritual life) has then a further dimension beyond that of a temporary absorption in spiritually androgynous states of consciousness. A larger task awaits us. We need to wake up to the deeper import of such purely positive non-polarized experiences, using them as a jumping-off point for deeper reflection on the very nature of experience itself. Living with others provides us with plenty of material for such deeper reflection, and alongside meditation can become an effective ground for breaking down the fundamental delusion that we are inherently separate from the rest of life.

In Beauty May We Live

Some people seem to be more sensitive than others to the effect their surroundings have on their state of mind, and they find it important to create a beautiful environment in which to live. On the surface, some may appear to be quite oblivious of their physical surroundings and not particularly bothered about the state of the decor or the cleanliness of the place. Of course, it's good to be flexible and adaptable and not overly dependent on needing our immediate environment to be a certain way. However, if we have a choice in the matter, it seems to benefit our state of mind to live in an environment that is aesthetically pleasing and where some care has gone into how the place is decorated and furnished. It may be that those who appear to be less bothered about the state of their immediate surroundings have simply become used to things being a certain way. This may be through force of circumstance or perhaps simply through not realizing that making some changes in their environment could benefit them.

One Buddhist commentator has suggested that for those people who have a propensity to aversion and focusing on the difficult, painful aspects of life, it is particularly helpful to live in a clean, aesthetically pleasing environment. This is presumably because there is less likelihood of one's surroundings triggering aversion. This is certainly true in my experience. For years on end I lived in sub-standard housing and had very little money, and in many respects my immediate environment was not very attractive. Nor were my mental states. One house even had polythene rather than glass in the windows in the kitchen because the local lads regularly lobbed bits of bricks through them. The carpets were old and tatty. There was little incentive to spend what little money we had on decoration when the walls were damp, rain dripped through the ceiling into the bedroom, and we were likely to be evicted at any moment.

I eventually became involved in teaching meditation and other classes at a new Dharma centre where great care had gone into the creation of a very beautiful meditation room and reception area. Indeed, a large community of men had worked on the entire building for many years and had lavished a great deal of love on it. They had transformed it from its derelict condition into something attractive and pleasing as well as serviceable. It was a new experience for me to be in such beautiful surroundings on a regular basis and it made me more aware of how my surroundings *did* affect me. In the reception room was a large mural of dark green forested slopes leading the eye to a beautiful lake with mountains in the distance. The morning sun cast its soft golden rays of light across the expanse of shimmering water, warmly drawing the onlooker into the scene. The colours and radiance reflecting back into the room through a skilful arrangement of lighting encouraged more relaxed, positive states of mind in me and no doubt in others, too, as they sat in the room. Gradually, I began to dream of creating a more beautiful environment for others and myself to live in.

So if we are in a position to do something about our immediate environment, it is well worth the effort. This can be a fruitful communal project, especially in communities where there is little or no overlap at work and opportunities to come together to share common tasks are more limited. Having a concrete project such as redecoration brings everyone together and creates further possibilities not only for getting to know one another but also for practising mutual helpfulness, patience, and cooperation.

If we have a meditation room in the house, we can use that as an opportunity to create an aesthetically pleasing environment in which to meditate. This will support our efforts to move beyond our everyday states of mind, which may not always be particularly positive, into more expansive, bright, entirely positive states of consciousness. Not that aesthetics should be confined to the meditation room. We can endeavour to make the whole house (and garden, if we have one) aesthetically pleasing. Moreover, making the communal areas attractive is likely to encourage community members to spend time together in them. Our environment *does* affect us, colours affect us, and so on. A house that is tastefully decorated and reasonably clean and tidy, where the material fabric of the place is taken care of, can conduce to positive mental states.

6

FOR THE BENEFIT OF ALL BEINGS

Thanks to the example of the Anuruddhas, we have covered a substantial amount of ground concerning communal living – and we haven't even quite finished hearing their story. Before we do that, let's briefly look back over what we have explored.

Communities are about people living together on the basis of common values or ideals and, for practising Buddhists, those ideals are embodied in the Three Jewels. We saw that communities can be a support to spiritual practice through the friendships we develop in living with one another. We then looked in more detail at what is involved in developing such a support to spiritual practice. Our heart needs to be engaged with living with others and there needs to be basic good will and friendliness. For communities to work, there is an ethical dimension to living with others, with everyone being willing and able to take responsibility for their actions and the effects of those actions, both on themselves and on others.

Living with others isn't necessarily easy. For many of us, it offers us both the greatest challenge and the greatest joy. One of the main challenges is certainly self-referentiality. But never fear, all is not gloomy – for there is a joy that arises through *overcoming* this tendency by thinking, feeling, and acting more and more with others in mind. We then looked at some areas of practice that can usefully be applied to a community of spiritual aspirants: simplicity of lifestyle, sharing of material resources, being environmentally aware, mutual responsibility for the practical running of the household, mutual cooperation, and meaningful communication. Finally, we briefly discussed meditation as a component of (and a real aid to) communal living and the helpfulness of creating an aesthetically pleasing environment in which to live.

So that's where we've been. Now to the other point. How *does* the Anuruddhas' story end? After the Anuruddhas have described in more detail to the Buddha how they are living together, he asks them a further question.

'Good, good, Anuruddha. But while you abide thus diligent, ardent, and resolute, have you attained any superhuman states, a distinction in knowledge and vision worthy of the noble ones, a comfortable abiding?'[15]

There are two versions of this part of the story in the ancient texts. Because of this, we can guess that the Buddha visited the Anuruddhas more than once, so one rendition is about an earlier visit, the other a later visit. In one version (or during the earlier visit), they are afflicted by various mental hindrances to their meditation and cannot sustain concentration. The Buddha sympathizes; he too has been through this in his quest for liberation. He describes in precise detail how he identified and eliminated each hindrance until he had fully mastered his mind and developed a depth and stability that conduced to the arising of 'knowledge and vision of things as they really are'. In this way, he gives them a clear overview of where they are heading, the hindrances that are likely to arise, and how to eliminate them.

When he visits again and asks the same question (in the other version), a quite different story unfolds. The Anuruddhas have now become adepts in meditation, moving at will from one superconscious state to another. Indeed, they too have now become Enlightened and he confirms their realization. These three young men certainly came a long way through living together and mutually supporting one another in their spiritual quest.

The story closes with a conversation between the Buddha and a spirit called Digha.[16] Whether or not we believe in beings with subtle bodies who occupy other planes of existence, the Buddha's response to what

Digha says is of interest as we conclude our exploration of community living. Digha tells the Buddha that

'It is a gain for the Vajjians, venerable sir, a great gain for the Vajjian people that the Tathagata, accomplished and fully Enlightened, dwells among them and these three clansmen, the venerable Anuruddha, the venerable Nandiya, and the venerable Kimbila!'[17]

The Buddha replies,

'So it is, Digha, so it is! And if the clan from which those three clansmen went forth from the home life into homelessness should remember them with confident heart, that would lead to the welfare and happiness of that clan for a long time. And if the retinue of the clan from which those three clansmen went forth ... the village from which they went forth ... the town from which they went forth ... the city from which they went forth ... the country from which those three clansmen went forth from the home life into homelessness should remember them with confident heart, that would lead to the welfare and happiness of that country for a long time. If all the nobles should remember those three clansmen with confident heart, that would lead to the welfare and happiness of the nobles for a long time. If all brahmins ... all merchants ... all workers should remember those three clansmen with confident heart, that would lead to the welfare and happiness of the workers for a long time. If the world with its gods, its Maras [demons], and its Brahmas, this generation with its recluses and brahmins, its princes and its people, should remember those three clansmen with confident heart, that would lead to the welfare and happiness of the world for a long time. See, Digha, how those three clansmen are practising for the welfare and happiness of the many, out of compassion for the world, for the good, welfare and happiness of gods and humans.'[18]

What we learn is that Anuruddha, Nandiya, and Kimbila, practising the Dharma together in the jungle and eventually gaining Enlightenment, will benefit all those who bring them to mind with 'confident heart'. They will benefit not only their immediate family and other relatives but also the whole village, town, city, and so forth. They will benefit people from all walks of life: labourers and merchants, kings and queens, religious practitioners of all beliefs. They will benefit all the various beings of this world on whatever plane of existence, be they gods, sprites, fairies, goblins, or humans. The Buddha is saying that the Dharma is universally significant and that *everyone* stands to gain if there are people dedicated to its practice who come to a direct experience of the truth of the teachings. He is saying that a spiritual community such as the one the Anuruddhas have developed benefits the world simply by its very existence and through others who are aware of its existence, bearing it in mind 'with confident heart'.

This might seem rather surprising (if not particularly relevant) for us now. We live in a world where the religious life is becoming increasingly marginalized, separate from the rest of life, even perhaps something of an escape from so-called real life. Buddhists are certainly sometimes perceived as escapists through their interest in meditation. Here, though, the Buddha is saying that people such as the Anuruddhas who uphold the spiritual values embodied in the Three Jewels and live a life dedicated to spiritual transformation can have a tonic effect on the wider community. How can this be? Is it still true today when society is so much more complex than in the time of the Buddha?

Initially, it might seem rather mysterious how such benefits can occur – but perhaps it isn't really that mysterious. After all, people are being affected by what they see and hear all the time, through advertisements, newspaper headlines, interactions in the street, and so on. So why should they not be affected by seeing or hearing of those leading a dedicated spiritual life which leads to total liberation of heart and mind? For example, in those locations where the FWBO has more established foci of activity in the form of Dharma centres, communities, and even work projects, we have noticed that these activities *do* start to impact positively on the local community. We know this because it is gradually communicated back to us by people who have started to pick up on what is happening: the positive atmosphere and so on. It's like a pebble being thrown into an expanse of water. The ripples generated by the pebble strike the surface of the water and spread out further and further. So whatever the form of activity generated by a number of people coming together is, it has an effect. Beneficial activity will have a beneficial effect.

The Buddha says the whole world may come to benefit from spiritual communities such as the Anuruddhas',
but in order to do so, people need to know of the
existence of such practitioners and, most importantly,
they need to bring them to mind with confident heart.
In other words, people need to put aside cynicism and
allow their hearts to respond to the good and the true,
so opening themselves more to their *own* capacity for
the good and true. This in turn will naturally give rise
to more positive attitudes in them and will lead to their
own and others' welfare and happiness.

The world would be in a very sorry state without any
dedicated spiritual practitioners, perhaps even more so
than it is already. Just imagine a world where the only
values were materialism and consumerism. What a grim
and stifling existence that would be. What a shallow
existence it would be. Unfortunately, this is not an impossible scenario. There are many people asking themselves what they can do to improve conditions in the
world. Many are doing what they can to alleviate the
physical and mental suffering of their fellow beings.

We may be wondering what we can do, or wondering
whether practising the Dharma will really help. We may
wonder whether living with other Dharma practitioners will really help. If we are wondering in this way, let
us take the Anuruddhas as our example on all levels. Let
us bring them to mind with confident heart and have
faith that we too may come to benefit the world through
living in spiritual fellowship with one another.

NOTES AND REFERENCES

1   The Western Buddhist Order (wbo) is a worldwide
    Buddhist spiritual community, founded by Urgyen
    Sangharakshita, which is developing a new Buddhist
    way of life, applying Buddhist principles to the modern
    world. The Friends of the Western Buddhist Order
    (fwbo) is the wider Buddhist movement that has the
    wbo as its nucleus.

2   The story of the Anuruddhas can be found at *Majjhima
    Nikāya* 128, the *Upakkilesa Sutta*. This translation used
    here is from *The Collection of the Middle Length Sayings*,
    trans. I.B. Horner, Pali Text Society, London 1976.

3   It wasn't long before some of the men and women
    coming along to these early fwbo retreats realized for
    themselves that continuing to live together outside the
    retreat situation might be one of the ways to generate
    such conditions. Thus began the first experiments in
    community living within the fwbo. That was back in
    the early 1970s. Since then many different fwbo
    communities have come into being and passed away, as

well as a number that have withstood the test of time and have been in existence for twenty years and more.

4   The traditional term for taking the Buddha, Dharma, and Sangha as one's refuge or reliance is 'Going for Refuge to the Three Jewels'. This means taking these as the ultimate and only reliable source of existential security and meaning. This is a dynamic act which takes place on deeper and deeper levels until Enlightenment is attained.

5   'Transcendental' here refers to experience that goes beyond the cyclic, mundane round of birth and death. It is the experience or viewpoint of an Enlightened being.

6   Published as *The Middle Length Discourses of the Buddha*, trans. Bhikkhu Ñāṇamoli and Bhikkhu Bodhi, Wisdom Publications, Boston 1995.

7   I.B. Horner, op. cit.

8   Bhikkhu Ñāṇamoli and Bhikhu Bodhi, op. cit.

9   Sangharakshita, 'Fifteen Points for Old (and New) Order Members', 1993.

10 I.B. Horner, op. cit.

11 In the Buddha's day there were, broadly speaking, only two options in terms of lifestyle: living in a family, either with one's birth family and other relatives, or with one's husband or wife and the husband's family; or leaving the household life completely and living the life of a wanderer. The Buddha had disciples living out their spiritual lives in both these contexts. Of the two options, the wandering life was considered the most supportive to spiritual practice, due to its simple, unencumbered nature, although it was clearly not going to be a way of life chosen by all or even the greater part

of his disciples. Such a way of life was supported by the wider society, whose members supplied the wanderers with food, clothing, and other basics. We can be sure that all the items mentioned in the Anuruddhas' simple community would have been donated to them. Not all wanderers were celibate, but the Buddha's disciples who adopted this lifestyle were expected to be so.

12 Sangharakshita, *The Ten Pillars of Buddhism*, Windhorse Publications, Birmingham 1996, p.67.

13 The five precepts are the most fundamental set of Buddhist ethical training principles and are practised within most schools of Buddhism. See Abhaya, *Living the Skilful Life: An Introduction to Buddhist Ethics*, Windhorse Publications, Birmingham 1996. The ten precepts are an extended set of ethical principles derived from the Buddha's teachings, see Sangharakshita, *The Ten Pillars of Buddhism*, Windhorse Publications, Birmingham 1996.

14 Sangharakshita, 'The Voice of Silence', published in *Complete Poems*, Windhorse Publications, Birmingham 1995.

15 Bhikkhu Ñāṇamoli and Bhikhu Bodhi, op. cit.

16 The ancient Indians still very much inhabited a world of gods and demons, ghosts and spirits, and various non-human beings regularly make their appearance in the Buddhist scriptures. Some early translators of these texts tended to cut out such references, assuming they were fanciful imaginings. However, this does a disservice to these ancient peoples. We also used to have angels and ghosts, goblins and sprites, in our

Western heritage until the scientific world view began to take over.

17 The Vajjians were the people who lived and ruled in the region where the Anuruddhas dwelt.

18 *Cūḷaghosinga Sutta, Majjhima Nikāya* 31, trans. Bhikkhu Ñāṇamoli and Bhikhu Bodhi, op. cit.

INDEX

The windhorse symbolizes the energy of the Enlightened mind carrying the truth of the Buddha's teachings to all corners of the world. On its back the windhorse bears three jewels representing the Buddha (the ideal of Enlightenment), the Dharma (the teachings of the Buddha), and the Sangha, (the community of the Buddha's enlightened followers). Windhorse Publications, through the medium of books, similarly takes these three jewels out to the world.

Windhorse Publications is a Buddhist publishing house, staffed by practising Buddhists. We place great emphasis on producing books of high quality, accessible and relevant to those interested in Buddhism at whatever level. Drawing on the whole range of the Buddhist tradition, Windhorse books include translations of traditional texts, commentaries, books that make links with Western culture and ways of life, biographies of Buddhists, and manuals on meditation.

As a charitable institution we welcome donations to help us continue our work. We also welcome manuscripts on aspects of Buddhism or meditation. For orders and catalogues contact

WINDHORSE PUBLICATIONS	WINDHORSE BOOKS	WEATHERHILL INC
11 PARK ROAD	P O BOX 574	41 MONROE TURNPIKE
BIRMINGHAM	NEWTON	TRUMBULL
B13 8AB	NSW 2042	CT 06611
UK	AUSTRALIA	USA

Windhorse Publications is an arm of the Friends of the Western Buddhist Order, which has more than sixty centres on five continents. Through these centres, members of the Western Buddhist Order offer regular programmes of events for the general public and for more experienced students. These include meditation classes, public talks, study on Buddhist themes and texts, and 'bodywork' classes such as t'ai chi, yoga, and massage. The FWBO also runs several retreat centres and the Karuna Trust, a fund-raising charity that supports social welfare projects in the slums and villages of India.

Many FWBO centres have residential spiritual communities and ethical businesses associated with them. Arts activities are encouraged too, as is the development of strong bonds of friendship between people who share the same ideals. In this way the FWBO is developing a unique approach to Buddhism, not simply as a set of techniques, less still as an exotic cultural interest, but as a creatively directed way of life for people living in the modern world.

If you would like more information about the FWBO please write to

LONDON BUDDHIST CENTRE	ARYALOKA
51 ROMAN ROAD	HEARTWOOD CIRCLE
LONDON	NEWMARKET
E2 OHU	NH 03857
UK	USA

ALSO FROM WINDHORSE

MAITREYABANDHU

THICKER THAN BLOOD:
FRIENDSHIP ON THE BUDDHIST PATH

This is a book about friendship – about the Buddhist ideals of spiritual
friendship and the author's personal experience. By turns moving, funny,
and inspirational, Maitreyabandhu's account is as compelling as a good novel.

   He does not shy away from those crucial and intimate issues that concern
us all – aloneness, sexuality, and falling in love. Maitreyabandhu urges us to
place friendship above every other human concern that can be imagined. By
the end of this book you might want to do just that.

256 pages
ISBN 1 899579 39 7
£8.50/$16.95

JINANANDA

MEDITATING

This is a guide to Buddhist meditation that is in sympathy with a modern
lifestyle. Accessible and thought-provoking, this books tells you what you
need to know to get started with meditation, and to keep going through the
ups and downs of everyday life. Realistic, witty, and very inspiring.

128 pages
ISBN 1 899579 07 9
£4.99/$9.95